French 101 French 102 French 103 French 104 French 201 French 300 French 400

A BOOK FOR LIFE!

Sans Détour

To the Point: French for English Speakers

> **A book that works with mathematical precision:**
>
> **it gives you the formula, then you have the answer!**

*An innovative grammar + 101 Conjugated Common Verbs
& 15 Charts that Outline every Area of French Grammar*

Priscilla & Gustavo Gac-Artigas.

TPB   **To the Point Books**

Printed in the United States
ISBN 0-9653060-1-1
Published by: **To the Point Books**
Library of Congress Catalog Card Number: 96-90413

TPB   1996

in the same series:

by Priscilla & Gustavo Gac-Artigas

Directo al grano:	"To the Point", Spanish for English Speakers
Sans Détour:	"To the Point", French for English Speakers
To the Point:	"Directo al grano", inglés para hispanohablantes
Directo al grano:	"Sans Détour", espagnol pour francophones
Sans Détour:	"Directo al grano", francés para hispanohablantes
To the Point:	"Sans Détour", anglais pour francophones

● **Sans Détour: French for English Speakers** is the perfect reference book for the beginner as well as the specialist: it is succint, easy to consult, clear, functional, precise and direct.

●**Sans Détour**: provides innovative formulas to solve, at a glance, the doubts about the use of French.

● **The series of Charts** [such as **Chart XII: Equivalence of Verbal Tenses between French, English and Spanish**] included in the book assure the mastery of the language targeted.

● **Sans Détour**, for French, **Directo al Grano**, for Spanish, and **To the Point**, for English give the authentic possibility of success in the clearest, fastest and effortless way possible.

● **Sans Détour**, is an indispensable and complete reference guide that puts language mastery at your fingertips!

Sans Détour.

Comme le dit le grand William, l'excellence du thé repose non pas sur l'heure de le prendre, mais sur la façon de le préparer; sur le fragile équilibre qui doit se produire entre l'eau bouillante et la coquette feuille qui se laisse posséder, mais...

mais, c'est la main experte du maître qui remuant délicatement avec une cuillère d'argent, trois fois le brevage, complétera la cérémonie pour offrir le céleste liquide aux esprits assoiffés qui l'attendent.

L'excellence du jambon fumé, déclara le manchot de Lépante, réside non pas dans la façon de le pendre mais dans le fragile équilibre qui doit se produire entre la brise insufflant la flamme et le vent déchaîné qui, avec la fumée, possède la frémissante viande, mais...

mais c'est la main experte du maître qui en coupera la fine tranche pour la poser sur les lèvres affamées qui attendent.

L'excellence de **Sans Détour** repose sur le fragile équilibre qui se produit entre la méthode d'enseignement utilisée et les fiches, complément nécessaire pour offrir les bases d'une nouvelle langue, mais...

mais, c'est la main experte du maître qui ajoutera la sauce, l'excellence du savoir faire, pour offrir aux affamés élèves qui l'attendent, le superbe régal.

Ô! Combien **Sans Détour** est loin de vouloir être une méthode ou une grammaire traditionnelle! La grandeur de **Sans Détour** repose sur le fait qu'il donne les fondements du français d'une façon claire, directe et fonctionnelle permettant aux étudiants de plonger dans les profondeurs de la méthode utilisée et émerger victorieux dans la nouvelle langue.

Priscilla & Gustavo Gac-Artigas

Dr. Priscilla C. Gac-Artigas, teaches Spanish and French at Monmouth University, New Jersey, USA. She studied at the University of Puerto Rico, Middlebury College, the Sorbonne and the department of Peninsular and Latin American studies of the University of Franche-Comté.

In the pedagogical field she is coauthor of: **Sans Détour**, for French, **Directo al grano**, for Spanish, **To the Point**, for English and: **The Bridge: from text to life**, an educational project conceived to improve the speaking of a foreign language.

She has been distinguished with the ELENA RALLE-94 prize awarded by the University of Franche-Comté to the research that contributes the best to the knowledge and difussion of Latin American Culture.

She has finished her first novel: CONVERSACIONES CON EL SER QUE SERÁS.

Gustavo Gac-Artigas, Chilean writer and theater director, is author of: TIEMPO DE SOÑAR, ¡E IL ORBO ERA RONDO!, DALIBÁ LA BRUJITA DEL CARIBE, EX-ILIADAS, UN ASESINATO CORRIENTE, SEIS HISTORIAS CARROLLTONESAS. In theater: EL PAÍS DE LAS LÁGRIMAS DE SANGRE, TE LLAMAMOS PABLO-PUEBLO, EL HUEVO DE COLÓN O COCA-COLA LES OFRECE UN VIAJE DE ENSUEÑOS POR AMÉRICA LATINA, CINCO SUSPIROS DE ETERNIDAD, DESCUBRIMENTANDO (DISCOVERINGS).

He is working on a new novel: EL SOLAR DE ADO.

He had been distinguished with the Poetry Park prize in the Netherlands and as honor professor by the Texas Christian University.

About his books, among others, the critic Severo Sarduy said:

about **TIEMPO**: *it is halogen, personal and even unique...*

about **DALIBÁ**: *we are in front of a completely strong and original literary genre between prose and poetry...*

and Edith Grossman said about **¡E IL ORBO!**: *I was impressed by the temporal game, the interpenetration of the historic, the mythological and the surrealistic...*

Contents

**Definite articles: they refer to specific
members of a group or class.**

-they are classified in definite and indefinite.

-they are either masculine or feminine, singular or plural according to the gender and
number of the noun with which they are used.

-in French the names of things (not only
living beings) have gender.

-the definite articles: *le, la, l'.., les* are equivalent to **the**.

	before a consonant	
	masc.	fem.
singular	**le**	**la**
plural	**les**	**les**
	before a vowel or a mute h	
singular	**l'**	**l' ***
plural	**les**	**les**

-* the def. art. *le* do not contract in front of:

un (numerical adj.)   *huit   onze   oui*

le huit janvier

-the masculine forms of the definite article
contract with the preposition *à*:

(*à* means: **to, in** or **at**)

$$à + le \rightarrow au$$

Je vais au théâtre.   I go to the theater.

$$à + les \rightarrow aux$$

Je parle aux étudiants. I speak to the students.

-do not contract with l':

$$à + l'... \rightarrow à \ l'...$$

$$à + la \rightarrow à \ la$$

J'étudie à l'université.   I study at the university.

Je vais à la bibliothèque. I go to the library.

contractions with *à*:

	before a consonant	
	masc.	fem.
singular	**au**	**à la**
plural	**aux**	**aux**
	before a vowel or a mute h	
singular	**à l'...**	**à l'...**
plural	**aux**	**aux**

-they contract also with the preposition *de*
(meaning from, about, of, some):

$$de + le \rightarrow du$$

$$de + les \rightarrow des$$

Je parle du nouveau roman de Gustavo

Gac-Artigas. *Je parle **des** romans de Gac-Artigas.*

-do not contract with **l'** :

$$de + l'... \rightarrow de\ l'...$$

$$de + la \rightarrow de\ la$$

*Je parle **de l'**oeuvre de Gustavo Gac-Artigas.*

*Je parle **de la** poésie de Rimbaud.*

Contractions with *de*:

	before a consonant	
	masc.	fem.
singular	**du**	**de la**
plural	**des**	**des**
	before a vowel or a mute h	
singular	**de l'**	**de l'**
plural	**des**	**des**

Uses:

-when the noun designates a person or an objet known or unique:

***La** Bastille fut une prison.*

***Le** soleil n'est pas une planète.*

-**to refer** to a noun in an ample or generic sense.

Les Renault (voitures) roulent bien.

Le lait est bon pour la santé.

-with nouns representing a broad category, group or profession.

***Les** écrivains doivent sauvegarder les rêves de l'humanité.*

-to make generalizations or to refer to abstract concepts: ***La** liberté, il faut la conquérir.*

-**in front of** the days of the week use *le* to indicate that an action is habitually done that day (when **each, on,** or **every** is meant):

***Le** mardi je fais mon marché.*

or that the action took place or will take place within a different period of time than the one of the enonciation:

*Elle est venue me voir **le** vendredi et est repartie **le** dimanche.*

-**to refer** to a specific day (ex.:last or next Tuesday) or to indicate an occurrence which takes place only once, the article is omitted:

Mardi prochain je partirai vers la France.

-**in front of** a date:

*Son anniversaire est **le** 6 mars.*

-**with** the seasons:

*C'est **l'**hiver, il neige.*

-**with** holidays: *le jour de l'an*

le 14 juillet

-it is not used before names of months:

Septembre c'est le mois de la rentrée.

-**after** the following verbs used in affirmative or negative to express a preference, likes or dislikes:

adorer   aimer   préférer

détester   apprécier.

*J'adore **les** voyages.*

*J'aime **la** bonne vie.*

*Je n'aime pas **l'**eau, je préfère **le** vin.*

*Ils détestent **le** fromage.*

-**to designate** a specific object:

*Donnez-moi **le** livre de français, s'il vous plaît.*

-**with** names of substances, materials and processes.

***Le** pétrole est le résultat de **la** transformation du matériel organique.*

-**before** titles and names modified by an adjective:

***Le** Président est un grand humaniste.*

***Le** Petit Robert est un grand dictionnaire.*

-it is not used when addressing a person directly or in front of **monsieur**, **madame** and **mademoiselle**:

Bonjour docteur Martin.

Bonsoir mademoiselle Duval.

-family names are pluralized in the definite article, not in the name:

*Téléphone **les** Dupont.*   Call the Duponts.

-**before** the name of languages, except after the verb **parler** (**unmodified**) and after the prepositions **en** and **de**:

***L'**italien est la langue de l'opéra, **le** français la langue de l'amour et **l'**anglais la langue du commerce.*

*Gustavo écrit **en** espagnol, la langue du merveilleux.*

*Vous parlez anglais, mais aussi très bien **le** français.*

-**before** the nouns used to identify national or local origin:

les Américains, les Parisiens

-**before** the first noun in a double-noun construction: ***la** classe de français*

***le** chef de famille   **le** maître d'hôtel*

-**with** fields of study:

*J'étudie **les** mathématiques, **la** physique et **la** biologie.*

-**with** parts of the body and clothing instead of the possessive adjective when it is clear who the possessor is:

*Elle se lave **les** mains, la belle française.*
*Elle a mal **aux** jambes.*

-if the noun is modified, the possessive adjective is used as in English:

*Elle se lave **ses** petites mains.*

-**with** expressions of rates and prices (per):

*Les fraises coûtent deux francs **le** kilo.*

-**to form** the superlative:

DALIBA, LA PETITE SORCIÈRE DES CARAÏBES *c'est son roman **le plus** poétique.*

*C'est son amie **la plus** fidèle.*

-**with** geographic names: continents, countries, provinces, regions, oceans, rivers, mountains. States follow the rules of countries:

***La** France et **l'**Espagne sont des pays voisins.*

***La** Seine traverse Paris.*

*Je connais bien **la** Georgie et **le** Texas.*

-it is not used with the names of cities or after **en** which is used with feminine place names:

*J'aime visiter **Avignon** quand je vais **en** France.*

exceptions: *Le Havre, Le Mans, La Haye, Le Caire, La Havane.*

-when the name of the city is modified the article is used:

Paris est merveilleux.

Le <u>vieux</u> Paris est merveilleux.

-it is omitted when a noun denoting profession, political belief, religion or nationality follows *être*:

Il est médecin.   John est américain.
Elle est démocrate.

-is omitted before each noun in a series:

Tout est à vendre: livres, cahiers, crayons, stylos.

> **Indefinite articles: they refer to any unspecified member of a general group or class.**

-the singular forms correspond to **a** and **an** and the plural forms to **some** or **a few** [restrictive quantity], in some cases to **about** or **around** [approximate quantity].

-they must agree in number and gender with the noun they modify:

	masc.	fem.	
singular	**un**	**une**	[a/an]
plural	**des**	**des**	[some, a few, about]

un étudiant ⇒ *des étudiants*
une étudiante ⇒ *des étudiantes*

Uses:

-they precede count nouns (nouns of objects you can count):

une banane ⇒ *des bananes*
un livre ⇒ *des livres*

-in a negative sentence they change to **de** or **d'** before the direct object, except for *être*, for **un** meaning **only one** or when opposing two nouns:

*Tu as **un** chien?*
*Non, je n'ai pas **de** chien.*
*C'est **un** chien?*
*Non, ce n'est pas **un** chien, c'est **un** unicorne.*
*Pierre n'a pas dit **un** mot.*
*Je ne veux pas **un** sandwich, je voudrais **une** quiche.*

-the indefinite article **des** is omitted after expressions of quantity:

beaucoup de	much/many
trop de	too much/many
une foule de	a lot of
un tas de	a pile of
assez de	enough

combien de	how much, how
autant de	as much/many
tant de	so much/many
peu de	few, little
un peu de	a little of
plus de	more
moins de	less, fewer

*Il boit trop **de** bières.*

*Très peu **d'**huîtres ont une perle.*

exceptions: *bien des (du, de la), la moitié des (du, de la), la plupart des (du, de la), encore des (du, de la), le plus grand nombre des.*

-the indefinite article is omitted when a noun denoting profession, political belief, religion or nationality follows **être**:

Je suis américaine.

Il est étudiant.

-but it is used when the noun that follows **être** is modified by an adjective:

*Je suis **une** <u>belle</u> américaine.*

*Victor Hugo est **un** poète <u>romantique</u>.*

*Nous sommes **de** <u>bons</u> étudiants.*

-it answers the questions:

Qui est là? Who is there?

Qui est-ce? Who is it?

Qu'est-ce que c'est? What is that?

with the pattern ***c'est* . . .** *c'est un/e* (it..is) or ***ce sont*** (they are) for the plural.

C'est un *avocat.*

C'est une *étudiante.*

Ce sont *des chats.*

-if ***Ce (C')*** is used in place of the pronouns ***il/s*** or ***elle/s*** when reference is made to nationality, political belief, religion or profession, the indefinite article is used: *Elle est française.*

C'est une *française.*

C'est un *médecin pauvre.*

Ce sont des *professeurs.*

-it is omitted in front of: **comme** (meaning: *en tant que* as a) **ni... ni** and after **avec** and **sans,** when it is used with an abstract noun:

*Il travaille **comme** journaliste.*

*Il regarda l'artiste peintre **sans** curiosité, plutôt **avec** sympathie.*

*Cela ne me fait **ni** chaud **ni** froid, dit l'ignorant.*

*Elle étudie SANS DETOUR **avec** enthousiasme.*

-and after a noun that is a complement of another noun:

   une belle chemise de nuit

   une maison de campagne

-and before each noun in a series:

   Il a acheté beaucoup d'instruments pour son magasin: pianos, violons, guitares, etc...

Partitive article: it refers to a part of a whole and it's formed of a combination of *de* + the definite article.

-it corresponds to **some** or **any**:

   *Je voudrais **des** fraises.*

-its use is obligatory in French to express any indefinite quantity:

   *Ils boivent **de l'**eau au repas.*

	singular	plural
masculine	**du/de l'**	**des**
feminine	**de la/de l'**	**des**

Uses: before an abstract noun to express an indefinite quantity, before a concrete noun referring to a quantity that cannot be counted or to a part of a whole:

   *Il a **de l'**amour pour la lecture.*

   *Elle aime manger **du** pain au chocolat.*

-ask yourself if you mean all the concept referred or only a part of it; if the answer is a part, use the partitive:

   *Pierre achète **de la** viande.*

   *Jean mange **du** pain.*

   *Je vous apporte **des** fruits.*

the partitive becomes ***de*** or ***d'***:

-in the negative except after ***être***:

   *Pierre n'achète pas **de** viande.*

   *Jean ne mange pas **d'** ananas.*

   *Je ne vous apporte pas **de** fruits.*

   *Ce n'est pas **de la** viande.*

-when used with a plural adjective that precedes a noun ***des*** becomes ***de***:

   Marie et Anne sont des filles. ⇒ *Elles sont **de** belles filles.*

Il a des amis ⇒ *Il a de bons amis.*

except when the group adjectif + noun is considered a compound noun.

> *des petits pois*
>
> *des petits fours*
>
> *des grands magasins*

-*de* instead of *des* is also used after expressions of quantity:

assez de	enough
beaucoup de	many
trop de	too much
tant de	so much
peu de	a little
plus de	more
moins de	less
un verre de	a cup of
une bouteille de	a bottle of
un kilo de	a kilo of
une douzaine de	a dozen of
un morceau de	a piece of
un mètre de	a meter of
une tranche de	a slice of

> *Je voudrais une douzaine d'oeufs, une tranche de jambon, un kilo de raisins et une bouteille de rouge, s'il vous plaît.*

exceptions: *bien des* (many of), *la plupart des* (most of).

> *Bien des jeunes étudient le français.*

-the adverbs of quantity *plusieurs* and *quelques* do not require the partitive:

> *J'ai mangé beaucoup de fruits.*
>
> *J'ai mangé quelques bananes et plusieurs fraises.*

-the partitive is omitted after the preposition *de*:

> *Le verre est plein de vin.*

-and after the preposition *sans*:

> *Il aime son café sans sucre.*

Gender of nouns:

-in French there are no neuters. All the nouns are either masculine or feminine.

Masculine nouns:

-names referring to beings of the male sex are masculine.

l'homme   *le singe*   *le dinosaure*

-names of months, days, seasons, holidays*, cardinal points and languages are always masculine:

le lundi   *le premier mai*   *le jour de l'an*
le nord   *le printemps*   *le français*

[*except la Toussaint et la Noël, but Noël accompanied by an adjective or in greetings is masculine.]

*Elle est venue pour **la** Noël.*
*Je vous souhaite **un bon** Noël.*

-cities are usually masculine except *Marseille, la Nouvelle Orléans, Bruxelles* that are considered feminine.

-names of trees and wines are masculine:

un *chêne*   **un** *sapin*
un *Beaujolais*   **un** *Côte du Rhône*

-nouns ending in a stressed syllable are masculine:

*le tabac, **un** tas, **le** bas, **le** plat.*

-names of colors and metals are masculine:

Le *rouge* et **le** *noir,* **l'**or, **l'**argent, **le** cuivre*

-items of clothing not ending in *e* are masculine:

le soulier   *le veston*

-most of the names borrowed from the English are masculine: **un** *parking,* **le** *week-end,* **le** *show*   **un** *meeting*

Common masculine endings:

-able: *câble*

-acle: *spectacle, miracle, pinacle*

-age: *récyclage, voyage, décalage, stage, étage, garage, village, visage, patinage, courage, message, fromage, passage, maquillage*

-al: *journal, récital, animal, cheval, signal, hôpital, local*

-ail: *travail, éventail*

-aire: *inventaire, maire, dictionnaire*

-eil: *soleil, oeil*

-asme: *enthousiasme, orgasme*

-at: *doctorat, soldat, consulat, chocolat*

-eau,: *bureau, châpeau, oiseau, morceau, gâteau, couteau, bateau, tableau, château, drapeau*

-ent: *parent, client, président, vent, argent, instrument*

-er: *danger, banquier, déjeuner, cuisinier, boulanger, épicier, charcutier, dîner*

-et: *objet, projet, buffet, cabinet*

-eur: *auteur, chanteur, vendeur, acteur, coeur, professeur, agriculteur, joueur, ingénieur, intérieur, moteur, radiateur*

-ien: *bien, technicien, mécanicien, Canadien, chien*

-in: *médecin, marin, cousin, voisin, vin*

-isme: *impérialisme, optimisme, nationalisme, racisme, fascisme, patriotisme*

-ment: *enseignement, mouvement, gouvernement, monument, bâtiment, établissement*

-oir: *soir, miroir, couloir, mouchoir, devoir, tiroir, arrossoir*

exceptions:

-able: *la table*

-age: *la page, une image, la cage, la plage, la rage*

-aire: *la grammaire*

-eau: *l'eau, la peau*

-ent: *une dent*

Feminine nouns:

-names referring to beings of the female sex are feminine:

   la *femme*   *l'abeille*   **la** *vache*

-flowers and fruits ending in **-e** are feminine, flowers and fruits ending in other letters than **-e**, are masculine:

   une *marguerite*, **une** *rose*, **une** *poire*, **une**

banane, **un** oeillet, **un** pétunia, **un** ananas
exception: *une* noix.

-countries ending in *-e* are feminine, except *le*
   Mexique, *le* Cambodge, *le* Mozambique et *le*
   Zaïre.

-continents ending in *-e* are also feminine:
   l'Europe   l'Asie

-names of cars are feminine:
   une Citroën   **une** Ford.

Common feminine endings:

*-ade: cascade, escapade, salade, parade,
estrade*
-aille: bataille
-aine: Américaine, douzaine,
*-aison: conjugaison, liaison, terminaison,
raison*
-ance: confiance, méfiance, enfance
-ande: viande, demande, commande
*-ée: cuillerée, matinée, journée, entrée,
année*
-eille: bouteille, vieille, oreille

-ence: patience, correspondence
-ère:boulangère, épicière,
*-esse: caresse, vitesse, paresse, finesse,
sagesse, richesse, jeunesse, maîtresse, prin-
cesse*
*-ette: allumette, alouette, baguette, cigarette,
maquette*
-euse: vendeuse, chanteuse, danseuse
*-ie: mélodie, maladie, crémerie, boucherie,
épicerie, compagnie, géographie*
*-ion: expression, exception, formation, respi-
ration, télévision, décision, discussion, profession, passion*
-té: bonté, liberté, nationalité, vérité
-te: route, croûte, brute
-tié: amitié, pitié
*-tion: addition, composition, occupation,
exception, question*
-trice: institutrice, actrice, directrice
-tude: attitude, étude, habitude, solitude
*-eur: candeur, chaleur, froideur, valeur,
peur, ferveur*
-oire: passoire, bouilloire
-que: banque, barque, marque, époque
*-ure: verdure, culture, agriculture, voiture,
bravure, nourriture*

and double consonant + e

la ville, la grippe, la sentinelle, la pomme, la classe, la personne, la femme, la richesse)

exceptions:

-ée: *le lycée, le musée*

-ie: *le génie, un incendie, un parapluie*

-ion: *un camion, un avion*

-té: *le député, le côté, l'été, le pâté, le traité*

-te: *le doute*

-que: *le manque*

-ence: *le silence*

-ette: *un squelette*

-eur: *l'honneur, le bonheur, le malheur*

-ure: *mercure, murmure*

-to form the feminine some nouns change the ending before adding **-e**.

Chart I. Nouns: masculine ⇒ feminine

er ⇒ ère	ier ⇒ ière	et ⇒ ette
eur⇒euse	ien ⇒ ienne	f ⇒ ve
on ⇒onne	oux ⇒ouse	teur ⇒ trice

un boulanger ⇒ *une* boulangère

un fermier ⇒ *une* fermière

un cadet ⇒ *une* cadette

un vendeur ⇒ *une* vendeuse

un chien ⇒ *une* chienne

un veuf ⇒ *une* veuve

un patron ⇒ *une* patronne

un époux ⇒ *une* épouse

un directeur ⇒ *une* directrice

Common nouns with a different form in the feminine:

un monsieur	*une* dame
un homme	*une* femme
le mari	*la* femme
le père	*la* mère
le frère	*la* soeur
le parrain	*la* marraine
le neveu	*la* nièce
un garçon	*une* fille
un oncle	*une* tante
un roi	*une* reine
un mâle	*une* femelle
le garçon	*la* serveuse

Nouns with different meaning for masculine and feminine:

un aide	**une** aide
male assistant	help
le critique	**la** critique
critic	criticism
le garde	**la** garde
guard/person	guard/action
le mode	**la** mode
method	fashion
un livre	**une** livre
book	pound
le poste	**la** poste
post	post office
l'office	**l'**office
office	pantry
le tour	**la** tour
turn/tour	tower
le voile	**la** voile
veil	sail

Masculine nouns used for masculine and feminine:

un ancêtre	un amateur
un ange	un assassin
un témoin	un bébé

un voyou   un vainqueur

Marie est **un bébé** très mignon.

-and in general all the nouns referring to professions previously associated with males:

un agent	un auteur
un chef	un compositeur
un écrivain	un juge
un médecin	un ministre
un peintre	un président
un professeur	

Simone de Beauvoir est **un** grand **écrivain**.

Feminine nouns used for feminine and masculine.

une bête	une brute
une étoile	sa majesté
une personne	une vedette
une victime	

Cet enfant est **une victime** de la société.
Cet homme est **une brute,** il bat sa femme.

Plural of nouns:

-it is formed by adding **-s**:

une table ⟹ des tables

-nouns ending in **-ou** form the plural by adding **-s**:

un clou ⟹ des clous

un trou ⟹ des trous

Seven exceptions:

bijou ⟹ bijoux

caillou ⟹ cailloux

chou ⟹ choux

genou ⟹ genoux

hibou ⟹ hiboux

joujou ⟹ joujoux

pou ⟹ poux

-singular nouns ending in **s**, **x** or **z** do not change their form in the plural:

le fils ⟹ les fils

un cours ⟹ des cours

le prix ⟹ les prix

une voix ⟹ des voix

le nez ⟹ les nez

-singular nouns ending in **-au**, **-eu** and **-eau** form their plural by adding **-x**:

le feu ⟹ les feux

un tableau ⟹ des tableaux

un cheveu ⟹ les cheveux

exception:

un pneu ⟹ des pneus

-most of singular nouns ending in **-al** form their plural by changing the ending to **-aux**:

un cheval ⟹ des chevaux

un journal ⟹ des journaux

un animal, un canal, un cordial, un hôpital, un radical

exceptions:

bal → bals

carnaval → carnavals

festival → festivals

final → finals

récital → récitals

régal → régals

-certain nouns ending in **-ail** form their plural by changing **ail** ⇒ **aux**:

bail	⇒	*b**aux***
corail	⇒	*cor**aux***
émail	⇒	*ém**aux***
travail	⇒	*trav**aux***
vitrail	⇒	*vitr**aux***

Nouns that have different forms in plural:

le ciel	⇒	*les cieux*
l'oeil	⇒	*les yeux*
***mon**sieur*	⇒	***mes**sieurs*
***ma**dame*	⇒	***mes**dames*
***ma**demoiselle*	⇒	***mes**demoiselles*
jeune homme	⇒	*jeunes gens*

Chart II.   Nouns: singular ⇒ plural

sing ⇒ **+ s**	**s = s**	**x = x**	**z = z**
au ⇒ + **x = aux**	**eu ⇒ +** **x = eux**	**eau ⇒ + x = eaux**	**al ⇒** **aux**

Nouns used only in the plural:

abois	at bay
alentours	environs
annales	annals
appointements	salary
archives	archives
confins	confines
décombres	debris
dépens	cost, expense
entrailles	entrails
fiançailles	engagement
frais	expenses
funérailles	obsequies
gens	people
menottes	handcuffs
moeurs	morals, habits
pleurs	tears, laments
pourparlers	discussions
représailles	reprisal
ténèbres	darkness
vivres	food supplies

*Il est arrivé aux **confins** de l'univers à la recherche de ses rêves.*

Nouns with different meanings in singular and plural:

singular	plural
affaire	*affaires*
business	trade
bien	*biens*
well	property
frais	*frais*
cool	fees, expenses
reste	*restes*
remainder	mortal remains

Plural of compound-nouns:

verb + noun	verb invariable
un **tire**-bouchon	des **tire**-bouchons
noun+noun	**both in plural**
un chou-fleur	des choux-fleurs
noun +adjectif	**both in plural**
un coffre-fort	des coffres-forts
adjectif +noun	**both in plural**
une longue-vue	des longues-vues
adjectif +adjectif	**both in plural**
un sourd-muet	des sourds-muets

Adjectives: they are modifiers that qualify, limit the meaning or make more definite a noun or pronoun.

-they are classified in: descriptive, numerical, possessive (stressed & unstressed),demonstrative, of quantity and indefinite.

Chart III. Place of the adjectives

precede ⇐ **noun** ⇒ follow		
numerical	**n**	descriptive
descriptive: when used for emphasis or as a poetic device.	**o**	
possessive unstressed	**u**	possessive stressed
demonstrative	**n**	
of quantity		
indefinite		

Descriptive adjectives (*qualificatifs*): they express a quality of the noun.

-they usually follow the noun they qualify, and must agree in gender and number with it:

*Les roses **blanches** sont belles.*

-**but** when used for emphasis or as a poetic device they can precede the noun:

*la **blanche** neige qui abrite mes rêves...*

Note: *beau, joli, petit, grand, gros, demi, prochain, dernier, nouveau* precede the noun.

*Un **beau** tableau, un **joli** garçon, un **petit** morceau, un **gros** mot, une **dernière** décep-tion, un **nouveau** départ*

Gender:

-in general to form the feminine add *e* to the masculine singular form:

grand	⇒	*grande*
fasciné	⇒	*fascinée*
uni	⇒	*unie*
intelligent	⇒	*intelligente*
émouvant	⇒	*émouvante*
idiot	⇒	*idiote*
civil	⇒	*civile*
gris	⇒	*grise*

exceptions:

favori	⇒	*favorite*
sot	⇒	*sotte*
gentil	⇒	*gentille*
bas	⇒	*basse*
gros	⇒	*grosse*
épais	⇒	*épaisse*

Adjectives ending in:

- *e:* don't change:

  facile   ⇒   *facile*

- *el* and *eil* add *le:*

  el ⇒ elle   **eil ⇒ eille**

  cruel   ⇒   *cruelle*

  pareil   ⇒   *pareille*

- *en, et, on, s*: double the consonant + *e*:

  en ⇒ enne   **et ⇒ ette**

  on ⇒ onne

  ancien ⇒ ancienne   coquet ⇒ coquette

  bon   ⇒ *bonne*

exceptions: *complet, discret, inquiet, secret, concret:* mark the vowel *è* before *t* & add *e*

       et ⇒ *ète*

  complet ⇒ *complète*

-*gu:* *add* *ë*

ambiguë   aiguë

-*er*: changes to *ère:*

  er   ⇒   *ère*

  fier   ⇒   *fière*

-*eux* , *eur* change to *euse:*

  eux ⇒ euse   eur ⇒ euse

  nombreux ⇒ *nombreuse*

  moqueur ⇒ *moqueuse*

exception: the comparative adjectives. (10)

  antérieur   →   *antérieure*

  extérieur   →   *extérieure*

  inférieur   →   *inférieure*

  intérieur   →   *intérieure*

  majeur   →   *majeure*

  meilleur   →   *meilleure*

  mineur   →   *mineure*

  postérieur   →   *postérieure*

  supérieur   →   *supérieure*

  ultérieur   →   *ultérieure*

-*eur* in front of *t* change to *rice:*

    teur   ⇒   **trice**

  provocateur ⇒ *provocatrice*

-*f* change to *ve:*   *f*   ⇒   *ve*

  actif   ⇒   *active*

  neuf   ⇒   *neuve*

sportif, agressif, négatif, naïf, imaginatif, impulsif, destructif, attentif, bref, vif

- *c* change to *che:*   *c*   ⇒   *che*

  blanc   ⇒   *blanche*

franc ⇒ *franche*

exceptions: *grec* ⇒ *grecque*

public ⇒ *publique   sec* ⇒ *sèche*

-nouns used as adjectives of color do not change:

    des chemises crème, des blouses orange.

exception: *rose et mauve*

    une robe mauve, des robes mauves.

-adjectives of color are invariable when modified by a noun or another *adjectif*:

    des chemises bleues

but *des chemises bleu clair* or *bleu foncé.*

-after *c'est, quelqu'un de, quelque chose de, personne de, rien de*, the adjective is not agreed:

    Mlle. Durand est quelqu'un d'important.

Chart IV.   Adjectives: masculine ⇒ feminine

masc ⇒ + e	e = e but é ⇒ ée	el ⇒ elle	eil ⇒ eille
en ⇒ enne	on ⇒ onne	et ⇒ tte	
er ⇒ ère	eux/eur ⇒ euse	f ⇒ ve	c ⇒ che

-the adjectives: *beau, nouveau, vieux, fou* and *mou* have a different form in the feminine:

singular

masculine:

before a consonant	before a vowel or mute h
beau	*bel*
nouveau	*nouvel*
vieux	*vieil*
fou	*fol*
mou	*mol*

feminine:

    belle

    nouvelle

    vieille

    folle

    molle

plural:

before a consonant, vowel or mute h:

masculine	feminine
beaux	*belles*
nouveaux	*nouvelles*
vieux	*vieilles*
foux	*folles*
moux	*molles*

-in general the plural of adjectives is formed by adding **-s** to the singular:

> *joli* ⇒ *jolis*
>
> *intelligente* ⇒ *intelligentes*

but adjectives ending in:

- **s** and **x**: do not change:

> *gros* ⇒ *gros*
>
> *heureux* ⇒ *heureux*

- **eau** add **x**:

> **eau** ⇒ **eaux**
>
> *beau* ⇒ *beaux*
>
> *nouveau* ⇒ *nouveaux*

- **al** change to **aux**:

> **al** ⇒ **aux**
>
> *royal* ⇒ *royaux*

exceptions: *banal* ⇒ *banals*

> *fatal/s*   *final/s*
>
> *glacial/s*   *natal/s*
>
> *naval/s*

-if a single adjective modifies two nouns, one masculine and one feminine, the adjective will be in the masculine plural form:

> *Mon frère et ma soeur sont gentils.*

-the adjective **demi** does not have a plural form.

-in front of a noun it is always invariable.

-it agrees in gender only after a noun showing a complete amount:

> *Une **demi**-heure.*
>
> *Un **demi**-kilo.*
>
> *Dix kilos et **demi**.*
>
> *Dix heures et **demie**.*

Chart V.   **Adjectives:**
singular ⇒ plural

sing ⇒ + s	s = s	x = x
eau ⇒ + x	al ⇒ aux	

Change of meaning:

-some adjectives change their meaning whether they precede (subjective consideration) or follow (objective consideration) the noun:

precede   **follow**

ancien   former   old

C'est l'ancien directeur de la troupe.

C'est une troupe ancienne.

brave   good   brave

Un brave homme.

Un homme brave.

certain   some   unquestionable

une certaine possibilité

une possibilité certaine

cher   dear   expensive

C'est un cher souvenir d'enfance.

C'est un souvenir très cher.

grand   great   big

C'est un grand homme.

C'est un homme grand.

même   the same   itself

C'est le même étudiant.

C'est l'étudiant lui-même.

nouveau   new-different   new-style

C'est ma nouvelle voiture.

C'est une voiture nouvelle.

pauvre   unfortunate   poor

Pauvre poète!

C'est un poète pauvre.

propre   own   clean

C'est ma propre histoire.

Ma chemise est propre.

seul   only one   alone/lonely

C'est le seul homme ici.

C'est un homme seul.

unique   only   unique

C'est l'unique étudiante hollandaise dans la salle.

C'est un étudiant unique!

vieux　old(long time)　elderly

*C'est mon **vieil** ami François.*

*C'est mon ami, le **vieux** François.*

Numerical adjectives: they express number and order.

-they are classified in: cardinal & ordinal. They precede the noun.

-**numerical cardinal**: they express number and are invariable with the exception of: ***un*** which agrees in gender with the noun

Ce roman a deux cent cinquante et une pages.

-et **vingt** et ***cent*** prennent un **s** quand ils sont multipliés

quatre-vingts (80=4 x 20) *trois cents* (3x100)

mais ils sont invariables quand ils sont suivis d'un autre chiffre.

quatre-vingt- treize   trois cent deux

-**numerical ordinal**: they express order.

premier/ère　→　first

deuxième　→　second

Possessive adjectives: they are modifiers used to denote possession.

single possession			
possessor	masculine	feminine	
je	**mon**	**ma**	my
tu	**ton**	**ta**	your
il/elle	**son**	**sa**	his/her/its
nous	**notre**	**notre**	our
vous	**votre**	**votre**	your
ils/elles	**leur**	**leur**	their

plural possessions masc./fem.		
je	**mes**	my
tu	**tes**	your
il/elle	**ses**	his/her/its
nous	**nos**	our
vous	**vos**	your
ils/elles	**leurs**	their

- ***mon**, **ton**, **son*** are used in front of a vowel or a mute h instead of ***ma**, **ta**, **sa*** to introduce a feminine noun:

***Mon** amie Pierrette, **ton** audace m'étonne.*

"De l'audace, encore de l'audace".

***Son** habitation est au troisième.*

-they must agree in number and gender with the noun modified.

-when *son, sa* and *ses* are used there is only one possessor who may possess one or several things:

le vélo à Pierre: ***son*** vélo

la voiture à Marie: ***sa*** voiture

les livres à Jany: ***ses*** livres

-when ***leur, leurs*** are used, there is more than one possessor that may possess one or several things:

Leur maison est belle. (La maison à Loulou et Fannou)

Leurs enfants sont beaux.

(Les enfants à Loulou et Fannou).

-Possessive adjectives are repeated before each noun in a series:

Mon père, ***ma*** mère et ***ta*** soeur sont allés au théâtre.

-with the parts of the body, when there is no doubt about the possessor, the definite article is used in place of the possessive adjective:

Elle a ***les*** mains sales.

-when there is doubt about who the possessor is, or if the part of the body is modified by an adjective or another expression, or if it is the subject of the sentence the possessive adjective is used:

Montre-moi ***tes*** pieds.

Tes mains sont sales.

mes grandes oreilles

exception: with the adjectives *droit* and *gauche:*

J'ai l'oreille gauche toute rouge.

-possessive adjectifs are also used in several expressions:

avoir ***son*** permis de conduire

faire ***sa*** toilette

faire ***son*** service militaire

passer ***son*** bac

prendre ***son*** temps

> **Demonstrative adjectives: they are modifiers used to point out a specific person, place, thing or idea and distinguish it from others of the same class, or to refer back to a noun already mentioned.**

Il était une fois une petite fille; cette fille...

	singular	
	masculine	feminine
	ce (cet) (this, that)	**cette** (this, that)
	plural	
	ces (these, those)	**ces** (these, those)

-they must agree in gender and number with the noun they modify. In English they correspond to **this, that** (singular: masc. or fem.), **these** and **those** (plural: masc. or fem.).

Cet is used before a masculine singular noun beginning with a vowel or mute h:

cet homme   *cet* appartement

-to make a direct comparison between two elements add *-ci* and *-là* after the nouns in order to make the contrast:

Ce tableau-ci est extraordinaire à différence de ce tableau-là.

-or to clarify the distance (in time or space) of the speaker from the object:

-ci (from *ici*)   this
-là (from *là-bas*)   that

Cette maison-ci est moins belle que cette maison-là. Laquelle? Celle qui est là-bas, à côté du pommier qui berce mes rêves.

Ce jour-là la terre a tremblé.

> **Interrogative adjectives: the interrogative *quel* (which, what) is used to ask questions when you want to identify one person, thing or a group of persons or things from a larger group.**

	masculine	feminine
sing.	**quel**	**quelle**
plural	**quels**	**quelles**

Quelle maison? Which house? (between many houses)

Sans Détour: French for English Speakers © Copyright Gac-Artigas 1994

-they must agree in gender and number with the noun they modify.

-they may be separated from the noun they modify when used with **être**:

> *Quelle est la maison?*

***Quel* et *Lequel*:** The interrogative pronoun *lequel* (which one) replaces *quel* + **the noun** it modifies:

> *Cette maison est belle.*
>
> *Quelle maison?* → **Laquelle**?

***Lequel* (*le + quel*)** agrees in gender and number with the noun modified:

	masculine	feminine
sing.	**lequel**	**laquelle**
plural	**lesquels**	**lesquelles**

Indefinite adjectives: they refer to an undefined quantity or number of things or beings. They are more indeterminate and imprecise than the other adjectives of quantity.

aucun/e	any
nul/le	not one
même	same
autre	other
certain/e	some
tel/le	such
plusieurs	several
chaque	each, every
quelque	some, a few
tout/e	all, any

*Je n'ai **aucune** nouvelle de lui.*

*Vous n'avez jamais vécu une **telle** aventure.*

***Chaque** matin il lit le journal.*

Chart VI. **Comparisons
of adjectives or adverbs.**

superiority
plus + adjective or adverb + **que**
more   than
inferiority
moins + adjective or adverb + **que**
less   than
equality
aussi + adjective or adverb + **que**
as   as
autant   **que**
as much/many   as
before numerals **que** is expressed by **de**

*Il est **plus** chic **que** son père.*

*Elle est **moins** belle **que** sa fille et pourtant
elle est la plus belle femme du monde.*

*Ils sont **aussi** heureux **que** leurs parents.*

*Je lui ai prêté **plus de** dix livres.*

- to compare how much of an action people
do, use: ***plus, moins*** or ***autant*** after the verb:

*Il mange **plus** que moi.*

*Il mange **moins** que moi.*

*Il mange **autant** que moi.*

-***plus de, autant de*** and ***moins de*** are used
before a noun to compare how much of something someone eats or drinks or has:

*J'ai **autant de** livres que toi.*

*Il a mangé **plus de** bananes que de prunes.*

-the adjectives ***bon, mauvais*** et ***petit*** have
irregular comparative forms:

bon	*meilleur/e/s/es*	(better)
mauvais	*plus mauvais*	
	pire (worst)	
petit	*plus petit* (in terms of size or measure)	
	moindre (the least, in terms of value or importance)	

-the adverbs ***bien*** et ***mal*** have also an irregular form:

bien	*mieux*
mal	*plus mal, pis*

-comparative adjectives used without the comparative sign (*plus, moins,* etc...) because they are already comparative:

meilleur ǂ *pire/moindre*

supérieur ǂ *inférieur*

antérieur ǂ *postérieur*

extérieur ǂ *intérieur*

majeur ǂ *mineur*

Superlative: is used to compare one or several persons or things to the rest of the group.

-it expresses the idea of the most, the least, the best, the worst.

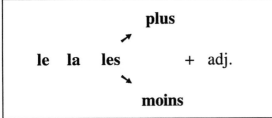

Paris c'est la plus belle ville du monde.

the most beautiful

-if the superlative follows the noun, the definite article is repeated:

C'est le garçon le plus doux du monde.

-if the noun follows the superlative, the definite article **le** is invariable:

C'est Marie qui a le plus d'idées.

-superlative adjectives used without the comparative or the superlative sign (***plus, moins, le plus, le moins,*** etc...) because they are already superlatives:

suprême, ultime, excellent, infini, immense.

The absolute superlative: is used to denote a high degree of quality without directly comparing the person or thing to anybody or anything else.

-it is formed by using an adverb modifying the adjective: *très, tout à fait, fort, bien,* etc...

C'est très facile.

Il est tout à fait exemplaire.

C'est fort probable.

-they express time, place, manner, degree, affirmation or negation.

-when they modify adjectives and other adverbs they are placed before the adjective or adverb modified:

*Il est **très** beau.*

-when they modify a verb they are placed after the verb, or after *pas, plus* and *jamais* in a negative sentence:

*Je n'aime pas **beaucoup** la viande.*

-in a compound tense the short adverbs are placed between the auxiliary verb and the past participle:

*Il a **bien** aimé le roman.*

-the adverbs of time and place: *aujourd'hui, demain, hier, ici, là, tôt, tard*, etc... are placed after the past participle in a compound tense:

*Elle est arrivée **tard**.*

*Il est arrivé **tôt** ce matin.*

*Il est parti **loin** d'ici, à la recherche de Cíbola.*

-when the verb is followed by an infinitive, the adverb precedes the infinitive:

*Elle va **beaucoup** aimer ce roman.*

> **Adverbs of manner**: they show a way of doing something or the way in which a thing is done or happens.

-they are formed by adding the suffix **-ment** to the feminine singular form of the adjectives that end in **a consonant.** The suffix **ment** is translated by the suffix **-ly** in English. They answer to the question *comment?* (-How?)

*froid   froide   ⇒   froide**ment***
*frais   fraîche   ⇒   fraîche**ment***
exceptions: *gentiment, brièvement, obscurément*

-if the adjective ends in *i, é, e* or *u*, the suffix **-ment** is added to the masculine form of the adjective:

*vrai   ⇒   vrai**ment***

aisé ⇒ aisé**ment**

absolu ⇒ absolu**ment**

facile ⇒ facile**ment**

exceptions: *énormément, intensément, pré-*

cisément, [fou ⇒ follement]

-if the adjective ends in **-ant** drop **-ant** and

add **-amment**:

courant ⇒ coura**mment**

-if it ends in **-ent** drop **-ent** and add **-emment**:

évident ⇒ évid**emment**

exception: *lentement*

-the adverbs of manner are generally placed

after the verb:

*Comme d'habitude elle me regarda **froide-**

ment, presque avec haine.*

-they can be placed at the beginning of a

sentence for emphasis:

***Lentement** l'auteur avançait vers la vieille*

pute serrant le couteau dans sa main gauche.

from A COMMON MURDER

by Gustavo Gac-Artigas

-other adverbs of manner:

bien: -meaning *très* in front of an adjective or

adverb:

*Elle est **bien** malade.*

-meaning ***beaucoup*** in front of a noun or in

front of ***d'autres***:

***Bien** d'autres ont vu ce film.*

-or meaning **well** after a verb:

*Il parle **bien** le français.*

mal opposite of ***bien***:

*Il parle **mal** l'espagnol.*

pis, comparative of ***mal*** in the sense of oppo-

site of ***mieux***:

*Il va de **mal** en **pis** ce garçon.*

comme comparative in the sense of **as**:

*Il parle **comme** un roi.*

ainsi	thus	*à tort*	wrongly
plutôt	rather	*exprès*	on purpose
vite	quickly	*volontiers*	willingly

Adverbs of time: they place the action or event in the time.

-they answer to the question *quand?* (when?):

hier yesterday	*avant-hier* the day before yesterday
aujourd'hui today	*demain* tomorrow
après-demain the day after tomorrow	*maintenant* now
aussitôt immediately	*longtemps* for a long time
autrefois previously	*jadis* long time ago
naguère lately	*désormais* from now on
toujours always	*souvent* often
quelquefois parfois sometimes	*soudain* suddenly
rarement rarely/seldom	*sans cesse* always
d'abord firstly	*ensuite* afterwards
tout de suite at once	*encore* again/still
tôt early	*tard* late
bientôt soon	*puis* then
déjà already	*alors* then
enfin finally	*depuis* since
plus tôt earlier	

D'abord j'irai à Paris, *ensuite* j'irai à Rome et *enfin* j'irai à Cíbola.

-*plus tôt*: means **earlier**.

   *Il est rentré **plus tôt**.*

do not confound with *plutôt* meaning **better or instead**:

   *Ne viens pas ce soir, viens **plutôt** demain matin.*

Adverbs of place: they place the action or event in the space.

-they answer to the question *où?* meaning:

où?   where?

   Où est-tu?

   Où vas-tu?

Par où?   where by?

   Par où est-il-passé?

D'où?   where from?

   D'où viens-tu?

some adverbs of place:

ici	‡	*là*	here-there
dessus	‡	*dessous*	over-below
au-dessus	‡	*au-dessous*	on-above

devant	≠	derrière	in front-behind
en avant	≠	en arrière	
dedans	≠	dehors	inside-outside
au-dedans	≠	au-dehors	inside-outside
loin	≠	près	far-near

ailleurs	partout
elsewhere	everywhere
là-bas	
over there	

y (always in front of the verb) means **dans cet endroit**:

> Il est à la fac?
>
> Oui, il **y** est.

en (always in front of the verb) means **de cet endroit**:

> Il vient de la fac?
>
> Oui, il **en** vient.

-they answer to the question **combien?** (How much/many?):

combien	
how many/much	
beaucoup	bien
much/many	many
guère	moins
little	less
assez	trop
enough	too much
tout	peu / un peu
totally	a little
plus more	si so
tant	autant
so much	as much/as many
très	davantage
very	more

-they answer to the question **combien?** (How much/many?):

> Elle était **toute** surprise, **toute** honteuse et **tout** intimidée. *

*tout is invariable except before a feminine adjective beginning in consonant or aspirated h for phonetical reasons.

beaucoup: is used with a verb, with a comparative or a noun preceded by **de**:

Elle a **beaucoup** voyagé.

Elle voyage **beaucoup plus que** son mari.

Elle fait **beaucoup de** voyages.

peu: is used with a verb or a noun preceded by **de**:

Elle fait **peu de** voyages.

-**très**: is used with an adjective or an adverb:

Il est **très** sympathique.

Il va **très** mal.

très ≠ trop (very ≠ too)

La soupe est **très** chaude.

La soupe est **trop** chaude.

Quantity adverbs that show a comparison:

plus, **moins**, **autant**, **aussi** (**+ que**)

-**autant** is always used with a verb or before a noun preceded by **de**:

Il a écrit **autant** de livres que toi.

-**aussi** is always used with an adjective or an adverb:

Il est **aussi** intelligent qu'elle.

tant, si, tellement are adverbs of quantity that express a big quantity:

Il fait **si** mauvais aujourd'hui!

J'ai **tellement** faim!

Adverbs of :doubt, affirmation, negation

doubt:

peut-être	probablement
maybe	probably
sans doute	apparemment
no doubt	apparently

affirmation:

oui	si
yes	yes
certainement	parfaitement
certainly	perfectly
bien sûr	sans doute
sure	certainly
soit	
all right	

negation:

non no	*ne... pas* no
pas du tout not at all	*nullement* not at all
jamais never	*personne* nobody
rien nothing	

Interrogative adverbs.

où? where?	*comment?* how?
pourquoi? why?	*quand?* when?
combien? how many? how much?	

PRONOUNS: ("for a noun") words used as a substitute of a noun.

> **Personal pronouns: pronouns used to substitute a noun or group of words already mentioned to avoid repetition.** They can be used as a subject, direct or indirect object of a verb, or as an object of a preposition.

Chart VII.   **Personal pronouns**

subject		direct object		indirect object	
je	I	**me**	me	**me**	(to) me
tu	you (informal)	**te**	you (informal)	**te**	(to) you (informal)
vous	you (formal)	**vous**	you (formal)	**vous**	(to) you (formal)
il/elle	he/she	**le/la**	him/her	**lui**	(to) him/her
nous	we	**nous**	us	**nous**	(to) us
vous	you all	**vous**	you plural	**vous**	(to) you plural
ils/elles	they (masc/fem)	**les**	them	**leur**	(to) them

stressed		reflexive	
moi	me/myself	**me**	(to) myself
toi	you/yourself (informal)	**te**	(to) yourself (informal)
vous	you/yourself (formal)	**vous**	(to) yourself (formal)
lui/elle/soi	him/himself her/herself one/oneself	**se**	(to) him/herself
nous	us/ourselves	**nous**	(to) ourselves
vous	you/yourselves (plural)	**vous**	(to) yourselves
eux/elles	them/themselves (masc/fem)	**se**	(to) themselves

je	I
tu	you (informal)
vous	you (formal)
il/elle	he/she
nous	we
vous	you all
ils/elles	they (masc/fem)

-they are usually placed before the verb.

-they are used as the subject of the verb:

Elle (Marie) prend son petit déjeuner.

Il (Jean) ne prend pas de café.

Ces plantes sont magnifiques et elles poussent partout.

Il becomes a neutral pronoun when used in impersonal sentences:

Il fait chaud.

Il neige.

-in the interrogative they follow the verb in a simple tense:

Ecrivez-vous des romans d'amour?

-in a compound tense they follow the auxiliary verb: *As-tu lu son dernier roman?*

*	**me**	me
*	**te**	you (informal)
*	**vous**	you (formal)
**	**le/la**	him/her
*	**nous**	us
*	**vous**	you plural
**	**les**	them

* refer to people   **refer to people or things

-they replace a noun preceded by a definite article, a possessive or a demonstrative adjective:

As-tu-rencontré Jean?

Non, je ne l'ai pas rencontré.

Il achètera la/ma/cette voiture.

Il l'achètera.

-they answer to the question **who? what?** in relation to the subject and verb:

Elle a lu le livre.   Elle l'a lu.

-they must agree in gender and number with the noun it's replaced and are placed before the conjugated verb in simple tenses:

Elle lit les livres.   *Elle les lit.*

-they can be used with *voici* and *voilà*:

Le/la *voici.* **Le/la** *voilà.*

-in front of words beginning with a vowel or mute h the singular forms become *m'.. t'... l'... s'...* :

Il écrit un nouveau roman.   *Il l'écrit.*

-in sentences with past participle they are placed before the auxiliary verb:

Je ne l'ai pas encore lu.

-in an affirmative command they follow the verb and are attached to it with a hyphen:

Etudiez-le.   *Invite-moi.*

(*me* becomes *moi*, *te* becomes *toi* after the verb).

-in the negative form they are placed before the verb without hyphen:

Ne l'étudiez pas.

Ne me parlez pas d'amour!, s'écria la folle.

-with a verb + infinitive they are placed before the infinitive:

Vous devez faire une composition. Vous devez la faire.

Indirect object pronouns: pronouns that precede the direct object and usually tell to whom? to what? or for whom? for what? **the action of the verb is done.**

me	(to) me
te	(to) you (informal)
vous	you (formal)
lui	(to) him/her
nous	(to) us
vous	(to) you plural
leur	(to) them

-they are always preceded by the preposition *à*.

exceptions:

after *être à quelqu'un, penser à qqn, songer à qqn, rêver à qqn, tenir à qqn...* and after the reflexive verbs followed by the preposition *à*, [*s'intéreser à, s'attacher à, s'adresser à...*], the stressed pronouns *moi, toi, lui, elle, nous, vous, eux, elles* are used.

Je songe à elle.   *Je m'intéresse à eux.*

-they are identical to the direct object pronouns except in the third person singular: *lui*

(used for: to/for him or to/for her) and in the third person plural **leur** (used for to/for them).
Lui and **leur** refer only to persons.

*Je parle à mes enfants.   Je **leur** parle.*

-direct and indirect object pronouns are placed before the verb except in an affirmative command where they are placed after, with hyphen:

Ils offrent des fleurs à leurs amies.
*Ils **les leur** offrent. Offrez-**les leur**!*

-in a negative sentence they come after **ne**:

*Ne **les leur** donnez pa!.*

Attention: some French verbs followed by *à* are often not introduced by *to* in English:
téléphoner à, dire à, demander à, offrir à, plaire à
on the contrary some French verbs take a direct object, whereas in English they require a preposition:

attendre	to wait for	*demander*	to ask for
écouter	to listen to	*espérer*	to hope for
regarder	to look at	*payer*	to pay for
chercher	to look for		

Reflexive pronouns: they indicate that the subject of a sentence does something to himself, herself, themselves. The subject of the action is also the recipient of the action. They are generally a direct object pronoun.

me	(to) myself
te	(to) yourself (informal)
vous	(to) yourself (formal)
se	(to) him/herself
nous	(to) ourselves
vous	(to) yourselves
se	(to) themselves

*Pierre **se** lève tôt.*

-they are an indirect object when the reflexive verb is followed by a direct object or with verbal forms as: *parler à, ècrire à, répondre à, téléphoner à...:*

*Pierre s'est acheté **une chemise**.*
*Ils **se** sont téléphoné.*

The pronouns: *y - en*.

Use *y* to replace a noun that is preceded by *à* when the noun refers to a thing or idea:

Pensez-vous à la question?

Oui, j'y pense.

-use *y* to replace a noun referring to a place preceded by any preposition other than *de*: (*à, à côté de, dans, en, en face de, près de, derrière, devant, entre, en face de, sous, sur, chez*)

Il est entré dans la maison?

Oui, il y est entré.

Je vais à Paris. J'y vais.

-the pronoun *y* is omitted before the future forms of the verb *aller*.

Vous irez en Europe? Oui, j'irai en été.

-use *en* to replace a noun referring to a thing or idea that is preceded by *de*:

Tu as beaucoup de projets?

Tu en as beaucoup?

-or to replace a noun referring to a place that is preceded by *de* (*en* means: from, out of, there):

Marie sort de la Comédie Française.

Elle en sort.

Je reviens de Paris.   J'en reviens.

-or to replace a noun preceded by *du, de la, de l', des* or any expression of quantity like *un/une, deux...* ou *un peu de, plusieurs, assez de, quelques, beaucoup de,* etc...

en means: of it, of them, some, any.

Il achète du pain.

Il en achète.

Tu as assez de pain?

Non, je n'en ai pas assez.

-they are placed before the verb:

Il m'en a toujours parlé.

-*y* & *en* are never used together except in the expression *il y a* where *en* precedes the verb:

Il y en a.

Il n'y en a pas.

Y en a-t-il?

Chart VIII. Order of the pronouns when used with other pronouns.

	①		②	
	me		le	
	te		la	
ne ⇒	se	⇒	les	⇒
	nous			
	vous			

③		④	⑤			
lui						
⇒ leur ⇒	y	⇒	en	⇒ verb	⇒	**pas**

*in compound tenses **pas** is placed immediately after the auxiliary verb.

**columns 1&3, 3&4 and 4&5 can never be used together, except 4&5 for *il y en a*.

affirmative imperative

    ↗ dir. obj. pron. ↘
verb   -y/-en
    ↘ ind. obj. pron. ↗

verb ⇒ dir.ob.pron ⇒ ind.ob.pron.

*Il ne **me le** donne pas.*

*Il ne **me l'**a pas donné.*

-in the case of a **verb + infinitive**, the pronouns precede the infinitive:

*Elle va **te le** donner demain.*

*Je ne veux <u>pas</u> **le lui** rendre.*

-in an affirmative command they are placed after the verb (and connected to it with a hyphen):

*Etudiez-**la**!*   *Allez-**y**!*   *Allez-**vous en**!*

Disjunctive or stressed pronouns: they are used to emphasize the subject or object.

moi	me/myself
toi	you/yourself (informal)
vous	you/yourself (formal)
lui/elle/soi*	him/himself her/herself one/oneself
nous	us/ourselves
vous	you/yourselves (plural)
eux/elles	them/themselves (masc/fem)

*soi is an indefinite form translated by oneself and it is used in connection with ***on***.

On doit toujours avoir un peu de sous sur soi.

-when used to emphasize the subject they are placed at the beginning or at the end of the sentence:

***Moi**? Je suis française, **moi**.*

-to emphasize the object they are placed at the end of the sentence:

*Pierre est un bon étudiant, **lui**.*

-they are used after ***c'est*** and ***ce sont***:

C'est *. . . moi/toi/lui/elle/nous/vous*

Ce sont *. . . eux/elles.*

or alone as a one word answer:

Qui est assis là?

Moi. Lui. Elle.

or compound with ***-même***

to mean my/your/him/her **-self**

      our/your/them   **-selves**

*Il s'est habillé **lui-même**.*

-they are used after ***et, ou, ni*** or a preposition:

*Pierre **et** moi.*

*Qui? Marie **ou** toi?*

*Elle pense **beaucoup à** lui.*

The neuter pronoun *le*:

Le is used as a neuter pronoun to replace an adjective, a clause or a whole sentence.

It's equivalent to **it** or **so** in English.

Croyez-vous que la criminalité va diminuer?

*Non, je ne **le** crois pas.*

> **Demonstrative pronouns: they substitute the noun and indicates their relation with subject, space and time.**

> **Definite demonstrative pronouns: they are used to single out the noun they replace. They must agree in number and gender with the noun replaced.**

---

	masculine	feminine
sing.	**celui**	**celle**
pl.	**ceux**	**celles**

-they are followed by a relative pronoun, a preposition or by ***-ci*** or ***-là***:

*Quelle est votre maison, **celle** de gauche ou **celle** de droite?*

-followed by a relative pronoun they can be translated for:

he (she) who, the one(s) who/that,

those who/that

*Regarde le tableau, **celui dont** je t'ai parlé.*

Look at the picture, **the one (that)** I told you about.

-followed by a preposition they can be translated for: **the one/s**

*Voici ma valise et **celle de Marie**.*

-followed by *-ci* they indicate relative proximity to the speaker and by *-là* they indicate relative distance from the speaker. They can be translated for:

this/that one

these those

***Ceux-ci** sont mes livres.*

***Celle-là** c'est ma voiture.*

Indefinite demonstrative pronouns: they refer to a general idea, statement or an object whose gender is unknown.

---

ceci	this
cela, ça [à l'oral]	that

---

*-**Ça** va?*

*-Oui, **ça** va. Et toi, **ça** va?*

*-Non, **ça** ne va pas.*

*-Avec toi, **ça** ne va jamais.*

Ce: neutre

-the demonstrative pronoun *ce* is generally used with *être* followed by a noun, an adjective, a pronoun or a superlative and can be translated for: **he, she, it, they** or **that**.

- *C'est* is used to precede a noun accompanied by its article, an adjective or any other modifier, or before a disjunctive pronoun:

***C'est** son mari.   **C'est** lui.*

***C'est** le plus grand écrivain de son temps.*

-with an adjective it is used to refer to an idea already mentioned:

J'ai fini d'écrire mon nouveau roman.

***C'est** merveilleux! (finir le roman)*

-use *il est* + **adjective** to introduce a new idea not mentioned before or when the antecedent is a specific person or thing:

J'ai fini d'écrire mon nouveau roman.

***Il est** merveilleux. (le roman)*

- *Ce sont* is used in the third person plural: *ce sont*:

***Ce sont** mes professeurs.   **Ce sont** eux.*

qui	who/whom
que	what
quoi	what
à qui	whose

qui is used to seek information about people

-when it is the subject it is placed at the beginning of the sentence:

Qui a lu IL ÉTAIT LE TEMPS DE RÊVER?

-when *qui* is an object it is also placed at the beginning of the sentence but use either *qui* or *qui est-ce que*:

Qui avez vous rencontré à Paris?

Qui est-ce que vous avez rencontré à Paris?

-when *qui* is the object of a preposition, the preposition becomes the first word of the question:

Avec qui est-ce que vous êtes allé en vacances?

-use *à qui* to denote ownership for persons:

A qui est ce livre?

que: the interrogative pronoun *que* (what) seeks information about things, actions or situations

-when *que* (what) is the subject of the question it must be used in the form:

qu'est-ce qui.

Qu'est-ce qui t'arrive?

-when *que* (what) is the object of the question it is followed by *est-ce que* or inversion to form the question:

Qu'est-ce que vous avez dit?

Qu'avez-vous dit, monsieur?

-when *que* (what) is the object of a preposition *quoi* is used immediately after the preposition and precedes either *est-ce que* or inversion:

De quoi vous mêlez-vous?

Avec quoi pourrais-je ouvrir cette boîte de Pandore?

antecedent	subj.	dir obj.
person	**qui**	**que**
	who	whom
things	**qui**	**que**
	that/which	that/which
indet.	**ce qui**	**ce que**
	what	what

-the simple relative pronouns *qui* and *que* are invariable in gender and number and they can replace names of persons or things.

- *qui* replaces the subject of the second sentence [qui is never contracted]:

La fille utilise les fiches.

La fille est une bonne étudiante.

*La fille **qui** utilise les fiches est une bonne étudiante.*

- *que* replaces the direct object of the relative clause [que contracts in front of a vowel or mute h]:

Je n'aime pas les gâteaux.

Jean m'a apporté un gâteau.

*Je n'aime pas le gâteau **que** Jean m'a ap-*

porté.

- *ce qui, ce que* and *ce dont* refer to ideas that do not have number or gender:

Ce qui m'embête c'est que la gloire soit arrivée si tard.

*On ne saura jamais **ce que** nos ennemis pensent.*

*On ne saura jamais **ce qu'**elle pense.*

Ce dont tu as besoin, tu l'auras.

Relative compound pronouns: they represent a person or thing already mentioned.

masc.	singular	plural
	lequel	**lesquels**
	duquel	**desquels**
	auquel	**auxquels**
fem.	singular	plural
	laquelle	**lesquelles**
	de laquelle	**desquelles**
	à laquelle	**auxquelles**

-the relative pronoun *dont* (of, about, of which, of whom, of where, that, replaces an object introduced by *de* + a noun) is used instead of: *de qui, duquel, de laquelle, desquels, desquelles*:

*Le livre **dont** je te parle est très intéressant.*

-use *de qui* or *duquel* instead of *dont* after the prepositions compound with *de: à côté de, auprès de, près de, au sujet de, loin de, à l'intérieur de, au cours de, au milieu de, à cause de, au-dessus de,* etc...

L'auteur **au sujet duquel** vous parlez est tout à fait extraordinaire.

-usually after a preposition use:

qui for people:

L'homme à **qui** je parle est grec.

lequel for things:

L'ordinateur avec **lequel** j'ai écrit mon livre est très puissant.

dont for both:

Enfin! Voici le texte **dont** nous avions besoin, écrit par l'auteur **dont** vous m'avez parlé.

Indefinite pronouns: they refer to a noun in an indeterminate and imprecise way.

-they are the indefinite adjectives
aucun/e   nul/le   autre   certain/e
tel/le   plusieurs tout/e

used as pronouns (without a noun) and the words:

autrui	the others
chacun	each one, everybody
quelqu'un	someone, somebody
	any one, anybody
on	one, people
personne	nobody
rien	nothing

Tu as des nouvelles de monsieur Martin? Non, **aucune**.

Possessive pronouns: pronouns that indicate possession.

---

	singular	plural
1 possessor	le mien/la mienne [mine] le tien/la tienne [yours] le sien/la sienne [his/hers/its]	les mien s/nes [mine] les tien s/nes [yours] les sien s/nes [his/hers/its]
several possess.	le/la nôtre [ours] le/la vôtre [yours] le/la leur [theirs]	les nôtres[ours] les vôtres[yours les leurs [theirs]

En parlant de livres: **les miens** à différence <u>du</u>* **sien** sont meilleurs que **les vôtres**, mais **le sien** est meilleur que **les leurs**.

*de le=du de les = des à le=au à les =aux

VERB: a verb is a word or a group of words that express action (*nager*/to swim) **or a state of being** (*être*/to be).

All French infinitives end in:

-er	-ir	-oir	or	-re

French regular verbs are conjugated by substituting personal endings that reflect the subject doing the action for the **-er, -ir**, **-oir** or **-re**.

Uses of the infinitive:

-as subject of the sentence:

> **Fumer** *est très mauvais pour la santé.*

-after a preposition: except with *en* that is used with the present participle:

> **Après** *étudier je ferai une sieste.*

-as a substitute for the imperative to give instructions or directions:

> *Ne pas* **déranger**.

-in exclamations or interrogative sentences to express doubt, wish and indignation:

> *Que* **dire!**
>
> *Qui* **croire?**
>
> *Toi,* **parler** *ainsi!*

-it is used after some verbs:

aimer to love	aller to go	désirer to desire
détester to hate	devoir to be obliged to / to owe	écouter to listen
entendre to hear	espérer to hope	faire to do
faillir to try	falloir to need	laisser to leave
oser to dare	penser to think	préférer to prefer
pouvoir can	regarder to look	savoir to know
sembler to seem	souhaiter to wish	valoir to be worth
voir to see	vouloir to want	etc...

> *Il a failli* **tomber**.
>
> *Elle doit* **étudier**.
>
> *Il faut* **rêver**.

Indicative: it is a mood used in ordinary objective statements.

-it is composed of the following tenses: present, present perfect, preterit, imperfect, plusperfect, past perfect, future, future perfect.

The present tense*: is used to express actions that occur in the actual moment, immediate future or habitually.

*tense means time.

It has different meanings: in addition to the simple present it can also express ongoing actions and it can be used to imply that an action will take place in the immediate future:

Je parle: I speak (as a habit)

Je parle: I am speaking (right now).

Je parle à la radio dans une heure.

I will talk in one hour.

Before a verb beginning with a vowel or mute h *je* changes to *j'*...:

J'habite rue Saint-Honoré.

Present tense of regular verbs ending in -er:

subject	stem +	ending
je		e
tu		es
il/elle		e
nous		ons
vous		ez
ils/elles		ent

chanter (to sing):

chante	*chantes*	*chante*
chantons	*chantez*	*chantent*

Irregular verbs ending in -er:

-there is only one:

aller   to go

singular	je	vais
	tu	vas
	il/elle	va
plural	nous	allons
	vous	allez
	ils/elles	vont

accent mark change:

e ⇒ è	é ⇒ è

-it occurs in the singular and third plural persons:

achet-er   *achèt* + er endings
to buy

gel-er   *gèl*   + er endings
to freeze

men-er   *mèn* + er endings
to carry

espér-er   *espè* + er endings
to hope

letter changes:

-double the consonant in the singular and third plural persons:

appel-er (to call) *appell* + er endings

jet-er (to throw) *jett*   + er endings

y ⇒ *i* in the singular and the third plural forms:

essay-er (to try) *essai* + er endings

pay-er (to pay) *pai*   + er endings

ennuy-er (to bore) *ennui* + er endings

envoy-er (to send) *envoi* + er endings

nettoy-er (to clean) *nettoi* + er endings

-letters that change only in the first person plural (before *o* in order to preserve the pronunciation):

$$c ⇒ ç$$

commenc-er (to begin) *començ + ons*

$$g ⇒ ge$$

mang-er   (to eat)   *mange + ons*

chang-er   (to exchange) *change + ons*

voyag-er   (to travel) *voyage + ons*

nag-er   (to swim) *nage + ons*

veng-er   (to avenge) *venge + ons*

Present tense of regular verbs ending in -ir.

subject	stem + ending
je	is
tu	is
il/elle	it
nous	issons
vous	issez
ils/elles	issent

regular:

fin-ir to finish	*chois-ir* to choose	*applaud-ir* to clap
rempl-ir to fill/refill	*bât-ir* to build	*réun-ir* to join again
réfléch-ir to consider	*réuss-ir* to succeed	*grand-ir* to grow /increase/magnify
nourr-ir to nourish	*obé-ir* to obey	*pun-ir* to punish

Irregular verbs ending in -ir or -oir:

avoir to have

singular	j'	ai
	tu	as
	il/elle	a
plural	nous	avons
	vous	avez
	ils/elles	ont

ven-ir   *ten-ir*

singular

ven → *vien* + -s, -s, -t

ten → *tien* + -s, -s, -t

plural

ven + -ons, -ez, *

ten + -ons, -ez, *

*third person: v + -iennent

t + -iennent

(stem= infinitive moins -enir)

venir to come	*tenir* to hold	*appartenir* to belong
entretenir to maintain	*obtenir* to obtain	*soutenir* to support
devenir to become	*parvenir* to reach/attain	*intervenir* to intervene
revenir to return	*se souvenir* to remember	*détenir* to detain
s'abstenir to refrain	*maintenir* to maintain	*contenir* to contain
	retenir to retain	

rec ev oir to receive

singular *reç* + ois ois oit

plural *recev* + ons ez *

third person pl. reç + oivent

apercevoir to notice	*percevoir* to perceive

part-ir

singular:

the singular forms of these verbs are formed by dropping the ending **-ir** of the infinitive + the consonant that precedes it and adding the appropriate endings to the remaining stem:

par **-tir** + **-s** **-s** **-t**

plural: drop the ending **-ir** and add the following endings:

part/-ir + **-ons** **-ez** **-ent**

partir to leave	*sentir* to feel/smell	*sortir* to go out
mentir to lie	*dormir* to sleep	*servir* to serve
départir to divide	*repartir* to distribute	*ressentir* to feel

sen/-t/-ir

singular   *sen* + endings

plural   *sent* + endings

sor/-t/-ir

singular   *sor* + endings

plural   *sort* + endings

men/-t/-ir

singular   *men* + endings

plural   *ment* + endings

dor/-m/-ir

singular   *dor* + endings

plural   *dorm*+ endings

ser/-v/-ir

singular   *ser* + endings

plural   *serv* + endings

offr-ir

offr   + **er** endings:

the stem + the endings of **-er** verbs.

singular   -e   -es   -e

plural   -ons -ez -ent

offr-ir to offer	*ouvr-ir* to open	*découvr-ir* to discover
couvr-ir to cover	*recouvr-ir* to cover up	*souffrir* to suffer
cour-ir to run	*cueill-ir* to pick	*accueillir* to welcome
	recueillir to gather	

ouvr-ir   *ouvr*   + **er** endings

découvr-ir   *découvr* + **er** end.

couvr-ir   *couvr*   + **er** en.

recouvr-ir   *recouvr* + **er** end.

souffr-ir   *souffr* + **er** en.

cueill-ir   *cueill* + **er** end.

mourir (to die): change ***our*** ⇒ ***eur*** in the singular and third plural persons. The third person singular adds a ***t*** (*il meurt*):

mourir   *meur* + ***-re*** ending

voir	*valoir*	*vouloir*
to see	to be worth	to want
pouvoir		*devoir*
to be able		to have to/owe

voir

vois	vois	voit
voyons	voyez	voient

valoir

vaux	vaux	vaut
valons	valez	valent

vouloir

veux	veux	veut
voulons	voulez	veulent

pouvoir

peux	peux	peut
pouvons	pouvez	peuvent

devoir

dois	dois	doit
devons	devez	doivent

-the verbs ***falloir, valoir mieux*** and ***pleuvoir*** are conjugated only in the impersonal **il** form:

il faut   **il vaut mieux**   **il pleut**

Il faut *que vous étudiez bien les fiches.*

Il vaut mieux *que tu écoutes attentivement.*

Il pleut *sur Santiago.*

Regular verbs ending in -re:

subject	stem + ending
je	s
tu	s
il/elle	-
nous	ons
vous	ez
ils/elles	ent

perd-re (to loose)   *perd*   + endings

rend-re (to return)   *rend*   + endings

attend-re (to wait)   *attend*   + endings

entend-re (to hear)   *entend*   + endings

vend-re (to sell)   *vend*   + endings

répond-re (to answer)   *répond*   + endings

confond-re (to confound) *confond* + endings

irregular verbs ending in -re

être (to be)

singular	je	suis
	tu	es
	il/elle	est
plural	nous	sommes
	vous	êtes
	ils/elles	sont

connaître

conna + **ir** regular endings

singular   *-is*   *-is*   **-ît**

plural   *-issons -issez -issent*

the stem is formed by dropping the suffix **ître** and adding the regular -ir endings.

-the third singular person takes a circumflex accent mark on the *î*:

connaître to know	*naître* to be born	*méconnaître* not to recognize
paraître to appear/seem	*apparaître* to appear	*disparaître* to disappear

li-re to read	*éli-re* to elect/choose	*reli-re* to re-read

singular

stem + *-s*   *-s*   *-t*

plural

stem + *-sons -sez -sent*

di-re (to say)   *contredi-re* (to contradict)

interdi-re (to forbid)   *predi-re* (to predict)

redi-re (to repeat) *

singular

stem + *-s*   *-s*   *-t*

plural

stem + *-sons -tes -sent*

* *maudire* (to curse) follow the pattern of *finir*.

écri-re to write	*réécri-re* to re-write	*décri-re* to describe
inscri-re to inscribe	*transcri-re* to transcribe	
sui-vre* to follow	*vi-vre* * to live/be alive	

*the stem is formed by dropping the suffix *-vre*

singular

stem + *-s*   *-s*   *-t*

plural

stem + *-vons -vez -vent*

fai-re to make/do	défai-re to unmake	refaire to do again
	satisfai-re to satisfy	

fai-s   fai-s   fai-t

fais-ons fai-tes font

pre/-nd/-re

singular

prend + -s   -s   -

plural

pre   + -nons -nez -nnent

pre/nd/-re to take	appre/nd/-re to learn
compre/nd/-re to understand	repre/nd/-re to recover
entrepre/nd/-re to undertake	surpre/nd/-re to surprise

Irregular verbs ending in -re or -ir:

courir to run	parcourir to travel through	rire to laugh
sourire to smile	rompre to break	corrompre to corrupt
	interrompre to interrupt	

cours cours court courons courez courent

-are conjugated like **-re** regular verbs at the difference that the third singular form adds **-t** to the stem. (*il court*):

cour-ir	cour	+	**-re** endings
parcour-ir	parcour	+	**-re** endings
ri-re	ri	+	**-re** endings
romp-re	romp	+	**-re** endings
interromp-re	interromp	+	**-re** endings

Irregular verbs ending in -re:
with double consonant:

the stem for the **singular** persons is formed by dropping the ending + one of the double consonants: *bat* ⇒ **tre**

for the **plural** forms the stem is formed by dropping just the ending: *batt* ⇒ re

singular *bat* + **-re** endings

plural   *batt* + **-re** endings

bat/-t/-re to beat	met/t/re to put/set/place
permet/t/re to permit	soumet/-t/-re to submit
combat/-t/-re to fight/combat	promet/-t/-re to promise
transmet/-t/-re to transmit	admet/-t/-re to admit

mets mets met mettons mettez mettent

-it is formed by dropping the **-ons** ending to the first plural form of the present indicative and adding *ant.*   *parlons* ⇒ *parlant*

-the English equivalent is the **-ing** form.

exceptions   *être*   ⇒   *étant*

avoir   ⇒   *ayant*

savoir   ⇒   *sachant*

-but generally, to express ongoing actions in the present time French prefers the use of the present tense or the expression: *être en train de...* rather than the present participle.

Qu'est-ce que tu fais? What are you doing?

Je mange. or *Je suis en train de manger.*

The present participle can be used:

-to express simultaneity with the main verb:

Voulant manger elle arrêta de travailler.

-as an adjective or as a verb.

As an adjective it agree in gender and number with the noun it modifies; as a verb it is invariable.

*L'histoire de Dalibá est une histoire **déli-**rante.*

Délirant dans sa baignoire Marat...

-it refers to a verb and has the same subject than that verb. It shows simultaneity of an action in relation to the verb. To reinforce the idea of simultaneity you can use *tout en:*

***Tout en** pleurant la mort de son mari elle riait de joie.*

-in general it expresses time:

*J'aime écrire **en écoutant** de la musique classique.* (**when**?... pendant que j'écoute...)

-it can also express the reason:

*Pierrette, **en jouant** trop aux cartes, s'est ruinée.* (**why**?... parce qu'elle joua...)

-it can also express the manner:

*Elle a quitté la salle **en pleurant**.*

(**how**?... en pleurant.)

-it can express a condition:

***En travaillant** vous aurez de bons résultats.*

(If... si vous travaillez...)

English -*ing*⇒French -*ant* [when introduced by the prepositon *en* or another prep. translatable by *en*; with the other preps. use the infinitive except with *après* that requires the perfect infinitive:

[*avoir* ou *être* à l'infinitif + part. passé].

*Réfléchissez **avant** de **parler**.*

Think **before talking**.

__Après avoir dit__ ça, elle est partie.

After saying that, she left.

> **Passé simple: presents a completed action in the past.**

-the action has **not** contact with the present.

-it is considered **as** something distant.

-it is a literary tense almost always used in third person singular.

*Honte de boire! **acheva** le buveur qui s'en-**ferma** définitivement dans le silence.*

from Le Petit Prince.

-the stem of regular verbs is formed by dropping the ending **of the** infinitive:

parler ⇒ *parl*

*fin**ir*** ⇒ *fin*

*ren**dre*** ⇒ *rend*

-**er** verbs.

stem	+	ending
je		ai
tu		as
il/elle		a
nous		âmes
vous		âtes
ils/elles		èrent

-**ir** verbs

stem	+	ending
je		is
tu		is
il/elle		it
nous		îmes
vous		îtes
ils/elles		irent

-**re** verbs

stem	+	ending
je		is
tu		is
il/elle		it
nous		îmes
vous		îtes
ils/elles		irent

Passé simple of irregular verbs: most irregular verbs form the passé simple from the past participle.

-Past participles ending in *u* (sound y):

us	us	ut	ûmes	ûtes	urent

avoir (to have)   eu → *j'eus*

boire (to drink)   bu → *je bus*

connaître (to know)   connu → *je connus*

courir (to run)   couru → *je courus*

devoir (to owe)   *dû* → *je dus*

paraître (to seem)   paru → *je parus*

falloir (to be necessary)   fallu → *je fallus*

lire (to read)   lu → *je lus*

plaire (to please)   plu → *je plus*

pleuvoir (to rain)   plu → *il plut*

pouvoir (to be able to do)   pu → *je pus*

recevoir (to receive)   reçu → *je reçus*

savoir (to know)   su → *je sus*

se taire (to be silent)   tu → *je me tus*

valoir (to be worth)   valu → *je valus*

vivre (to live/be alive)   vécu → *je vécus*

vouloir (to want)   voulu → *je voulus*

-Past participles ending in *i* (sound i):

is	is	it	îmes	îtes	irent

asseoir (to sit down)   assis → *j'assis*

dire (to say)   dit → *je dis*

dormir (to sleep)   dormi → *je dormis*

mettre (to put)   mis → *je mis*

ins	ins	int	înmes	întes	inrent

tenir, venir and their compounds:

tenir → *tins*   *venir* → *vins*

revenir → *revins*

-verbs that do not form their passé simple from the past participle:

être - fus   *écrire - écrivis*   *faire - fis*

mourir - mourus   *naître - naquis*   *voir - vis*

Passé récent: it expresses an action completed in the near past.

-it is formed with the present of:

    venir + de + infinitive

Je viens de finir mon nouveau roman.

-it is a compound tense formed as follows:

present of auxiliary verb (*avoir* or *être*) + past participle

J'ai été à Avignon l'été dernier.

in negative sentences:

ne/n' ⇒present of auxiliary verb ⇒ *pas* ⇒ past participle.

je n'⇒*ai* ⇒*pas* ⇒ *été*...

-the most of the French verbs form the passé composé with the present tense of the auxiliary verb *avoir* + the past participle.

The past participle:

-for regular verbs it is formed by replacing the infinitive endings with the past participle ending.

Past participle endings:

of regular verbs ending in		
-er	→	-é
-ir	→	-i
-re	→	-u

of irregular verbs:

apprendre (to learn)	appris
avoir (to have)	eu
battre (to fight)	battu
boire (to drink)	bu
comprendre (to understand)	compris
conduire (to drive)	conduit
connaître (to know)	connu
courir (to run)	couru
couvrir (to cover)	couvert
croire (to believe)	cru
devoir (to owe)	dû
dire (to say)	dit
écrire (to write)	écrit
être (to be)	été
faire (to do/make)	fait
falloir (to be necessary)	fallu
lire (to read)	lu
mettre (to put)	mis
mourir (to die)	mort
naître (to be born)	né
ouvrir (to open)	ouvert
plaire (to please)	plu
pleuvoir (to rain)	plu
prendre (to take)	pris
recevoir (to receive)	reçu
rire (to laugh)	ri
souffrir (to suffer)	souffert
venir (to come)	venu
vivre (to live/be alive)	vécu
voir (to see)	vu

-the past participle of verbs conjugated with the auxiliary *avoir* agrees in gender and number with the direct object pronoun only when it is placed in front of the verb:

La lettre?   Je l'ai déjà écrite.

- there is no agreement with *y, dont* or *en*:

De belles statues?

Il en a vu.

-**with *être*** the past participle agrees in gender and number with the subject:

Elle est arrivée à Paris vers minuit.

-the past participle of the reflexive and reciprocal verbs agrees in gender and number with a preceding direct object:

Marie s'est lavée. (s':dir.obj)

-when the direct object follows the verb there is no agreement:

Marie s'est lavé les cheveux.

(*s'*:ind. obj. *les cheveux* :d.o)

[* The verbs: *monter, descendre, sortir, rentrer, retourner* and *passer* use *avoir* when they take a direct object.

J'ai descendu l'escalier.

J'ai sorti ma voiture du garage.

Nous avons passé de bonnes vacances.

Verbs that form the passé composé with *être*

aller (to go)
Je suis allé à la gare,
apparaître (to appear)
le train est apparu,
arriver (to arrive)
il est arrivé à minuit pile.
descendre (to descend)
Elle est descendue lentement de la voiture,
venir (to come)
elle est venue vers moi,
entrer (to enter)
et elle est entrée dans ma vie.
naître (to be born)
Cette nuit-là un amour est né.
mourir (to die)
Mon passé est mort dans ses bras et
partir (to leave)
nous sommes partis vers l'avenir.
rester (to stay)
La gare est restée seule,
retourner (to return)
nous ne sommes jamais retournés à cette gare
tomber (to fall)
où à minuit pile nous sommes tombés amoureux.
the end.
Monter (to climb) et **sortir** (to go out)? C'est une autre histoire.
Gustavo Gac-Artigas

and their compounds

+ *passer, décéder* and all the reflexive verbs.

-the imperfect is formed by dropping the **-ons** from the first person plural of the present indicative and adding the endings of the imperfect:

singular	je	-ais
	tu	-ais
	il/elle/on	-ait
plural	nous	-ions
	vous	-iez
	ils/elles	-aient

-all the verbs are regular in the imperfect except *être* (to be):

j'étais	nous étions
tu étais	vous étiez
il/elle/on était	ils/elles étaient

Verbs with spelling changes in the imperfect. [first and second plural persons.]

-cer and *-ger* verbs

-çais	-geais
-çais	-geais
-çait	-geait
-cions	-gions [*ç⇒c ge⇒gi]
-ciez	-giez [*ç⇒c ge⇒gi]
-çaient	-geaient

[*c:before i/e sounds s, for that reason the cedilla is not needed; g: before i/e sounds ʒ, for that reason the e is not needed].

uses:

-it expresses habitual or repeated actions in the past, there is no clear indication of the time of beginning or ending of these actions.

-in English it is equivalent to: was doing, used to do or did, would + infinitive.

-it expresses a wish, suggestion or supposition in *si* sentences:

Et si vous partiez tout de suite?

-it is used to describe simultaneous actions in the past:

Elle lisait sur mon épaule pendant que j'écrivais UN ASSASSINAT ORDINAIRE.

Elle n'a jamais su qui était l'assassin et qui la victime, monsieur le juge.

from Un Assassinat Ordinaire
by Gustavo Gac-Artigas

-it is used to tell time and to express age in the past:

Il était huit heures quand le drame a eu lieu.

Melina avait trois ans quand elle a commencé à rêver tout éveillée.

Imperfect ≠ passé composé

---

imperfect: it is used to describe past actions or states that where not completed.

-what was going on or how things were.

-it provides a description of the scenario.

passé composé: it is used to express a completed action in the past.

-actions are not continuous or descriptive.

-they don't provide the background of the scenario.

-they give the completed actions developping the story line.

Je prenais ma douche...

quand il a frappé à la porte.

imperfect: it's the insurance agent after the accident. What was going on? What was the situation? How were things or people?

passé composé: it's the gossip that arrives a minute after the accident.

What happened? What did people do? action - not details.

Past perfect: is a tense used to express or describe an action that was completed before another action in the past.

-it is formed with the imperfect of *être* or *avoir* + past participle.

Il était sorti ce soir.

Nous avions étudié la leçon.

-it is used to express an action that was completed before another action in the past:

Nous sommes allés au restaurant dont tu nous avais parlé.

Quand ils ont fini l'examen, ils étaient épuisés.

-it is used to describe a condition or a state existing in the past before another condition or state:

*Il **était devenu** célèbre même avant la publication de son deuxième roman.*

-with the preposition *si* it expresses the ir-reality of a past event:

*Si tu **étais allé** chez le médecin hier, tu te sentirais mieux aujourd'hui.*

Future tense: is a tense that expresses actions that have not yet occurred.

-it is equivalent to the English: **will/shall + verb**: *Je **finirai** mes études dans trois ans.*

-it can express the idea of a near or a distant future action:

*Il **pleuvra** ce soir.*

*Nous **partirons** en vacances l'été prochain.*

-it can be used instead of the imperative to soften a command:

*Vous m'**apporterez** (apportez-moi) le rapport lundi prochain.*

Formation:

-it is formed by adding to the infinitive the following endings:

singular	je	-ai
	tu	-as
	il/elle/on	-a
plural	nous	-ons
	vous	-ez
	ils/elles	-ont

-for the **-re** verbs the final **-e** must be dropped before adding the endings.

(except for *faire*: ⇒ *fer* + endings.)

-the verbs with stem changes in the present have the same changes in the future:

accent mark change: e ⇒ è

-it occurs in all the persons.

achet-er (to buy)	*achèter* + endings
amen-er (to carry)	*amèner* + endings
geler (to freeze)	*gèler* + endings

letter changes:

regular **-er** verbs double the consonant in all the persons:

appel-er (to call)	*appeller* + endings
jet-er (to throw)	*jetter* + endings

exceptions: *acheter* et *geler*

$y \Rightarrow i$ in the singular and the third plural forms:

essay-er (to try) *essaier* + endings

pay-er (to pay) *paier* + endings

Verbs with irregular stem in the future

avoir (to have)	aur-	**plus**	endings
savoir (to know)	saur-		endings
falloir (to be necessary)	faudr-		endings
valoir (to be worth)	vaudr-		endings
devoir (to owe)	devr-		endings
recevoir (to receive)	recevr-		endings
pleuvoir (to rain)	pleuvr-		endings
être (to be)	ser-		endings
faire (to do/make)	fer-		endings
aller (to go)	ir-		endings
acquérir (to acquire)	acquerr-		endings
conquérir (to conquer)	conquerr-		endings
envoyer (to send)	enverr-		endings
voir (to see)	verr-		endings
courir (to run)	courr-		endings
mourir (to die)	mourr-		endings
pouvoir (to be able to do)	pourr-		endings
obtenir (to obtain)	obtiendr-		endings
tenir (to have)	tiendr-		endings
venir (to come)	viendr-		endings
vouloir (to want)	voudr-		endings

The future perfect: is a compound tense used to express that an action in the future will take place, and be completed, after another action in the future have taken place.

-it is formed with the future tense of the auxiliary verb and the past participle of the main verb.

future of *avoir* or *être* + *participe passé*

will have + **past participle**

Tu finiras de chercher Cíbola quand tu auras appris à déchiffrer les chanchogrammes, dit Sempronio à Chavalillo.

from ¡E IL ORBO ERA RONDO!

by Gustavo Gac-Artigas

-when used alone it expresses a completed action in a precise moment of the future specified in general by a time expression:

Dans une semaine j'aurai fini mon roman.

-it can express probability:

Jean n'est pas venu; il aura peut-être eu un accident?

-it is always used after the conjunctions: *quand, lorsque* (when/where), *dès que, aussitôt que* (as soon as), *après que* (after...) and *tant que* (as long as) when a future idea is implied. The action introduced by these expressions has not yet taken place.

Je passerai te voir dès que j'aurai fini le rapport.

Tant que je n'aurai pas fini les livres je ne serai pas tranquille.

The near future: is used to express actions or events in a near future.

-it is formed with the present tense of

aller + infinitive:

Nous allons déménager.

-the English equivalent is:

to be going + infinitive

Allez-vous étudier plus tard?

-it presents as certain an action that will take place in a distant future:

Dans cinq ans nous allons fêter nos noces d'argent.

Expressions of future time:

-with *demain* (tomorrow):

demain matin   demain après-midi
demain soir

-with *prochain* (next):

lundi prochain   la semaine prochaine
le mois prochain   l'année prochaine
seasons: *l'été prochain.*

-in *si* (if) clauses:

dependent clause: present

main clause: future/imperative

Si vous me donnez la réponse je partirai heureuse.

main clause: future   *quand:* future perfect.

Je partirai quand vous m'aurez donné la réponse.

The conditional: it is a mood that expresses a hypothetical situation that can or can not take place or that is subject to some condition before it can take place in sentences including a *si* (if) clause.

Si j'étais à votre place j'étudierais les fiches.

Vous auriez de meilleurs résultats si vous étudiez les fiches.

It has two tenses: **present** and **past**.

Present conditional: to form the present conditional use the infinitive as the stem and add the following endings:

singular	je	-ais
	tu	-ais
	il/elle/on	-ait
plural	nous	-ions
	vous	-iez
	ils/elles	-aient

for -re verbs drop the **-e** from the infinitive form and add the endings.

-exception: *faire* (to make/do) = ⇒ *fer* + endings

for irregular verbs use the stem of the future tense.

avoir (to have)	*aur-*	+ endings
savoir (to know)	*saur-*	+ endings
falloir (to be necessary)	*faudr-*	+ endings
valoir (to be worth)	*vaudr-*	+ endings
devoir (to owe)	*devr-*	+ endings
recevoir (to receive)	*recevr-*	+ endings
pleuvoir (to rain)	*pleuvr-*	+ endings
être (to be)	*ser-*	+ endings
faire (to make/do)	*fer-*	+ endings
aller (to go)	*ir-*	+ endings
acquérir (to purchase)	*acquerr-*	+ endings
conquérir (to conquer)	*conquerr-*	+ endings
envoyer (to send)	*enverr-*	+ endings
voir (to see)	*verr-*	+ endings
courir (to run)	*courr-*	+ endings
mourir (to die)	*mourr-*	+ endings
pouvoir (to be able to do)	*pourr-*	+ endings
obtenir (to obtain)	*obtiendr-*	+ endings
tenir (to have)	*tiendr-*	+ endings
venir (to come)	*viendr-*	+ endings
vouloir (to want)	*voudr-*	+ endings

Uses:

-it is used to tell what would happen in future actions in reference to the past:

Hier on m'a dit que ma fille serait une grande pianiste.

-it is also used to soften requests, statements or commands:

Usually with: *pouvoir - vouloir - aimer*
Pourriez-vous garder silence?
Je voudrais avoir une belle maison.

-to express a wish or a dream:

J'aimerais bien aller me promener.

-to express an information whose accuracy is not guaranteed:

Le témoin oculaire dit qu'il y aurait au moins une trentaine de morts.

-to express an imaginary event:

Elle les voyait déjà: ils marcheraient la main dans la main vers l'avenir.

-to express a possibility or supposition:

Va le voir aujourd'hui, demain ce serait trop tard.

-in *si* clauses where the condition is expressed with the imperfect:

S'il n'était pas marié, je l'épouserais.

Conditional perfect: is used to express what would have occur at one moment in the past.

-in English it can be translated by **would have**.

-it is formed with the present conditional of the auxiliary verb (*avoir - être*) and the past participle of the verb.

	avoir (to have)	**être** (to be)
je (j')	aurais	serais
tu	aurais	serais
il/elle	aurait	serait
nous	aurions	serions
vous	auriez	seriez
ils/elles	auraient	seraient

Elle serait allée en France si elle avait eu le temps.

Sans Détour: French for English Speakers © Copyright Gac-Artigas 1994

- it is used to express regrets or indignation:

J'aurais bien voulu finir mes études, mais je n'ai pas pu.

Chart IX. Agreement between tenses in hypothetical systems:

condition   **résultat**

présent:	**futur:**
Si j'ai le temps...	*...j'irai vous voir.*
imparfait:	**conditionnel présent:**
Si j'avais le temps...	*...j'irais vous voir.*
plus-que-parfait:	**conditionnel passé:**
Si j'avais eu le temps...	*...je serais allé vous voir.*

Subjunctive: It's a verbal mood (the attitude the speaker has toward a fact or action): primarily it indicates that something is not a fact or that something should happen: **if** . . .

-it has four tenses: present, past/present perfect, imperfect and pluperfect/past perfect.

It is used to express an attitude, feelings, beliefs or opinions toward an idea or fact; to express statements or questions that reflect doubt, desire, emotion, hope, possibility, influence, lack of existence, or uncertainty.

-it represents an act or state as contingent or hypothetical, actions viewed subjectively, or subordinate statements.

-it is usually subordinate to another dominating idea, the independent clause, that contains the verb in the indicative mood.

-the dependent clause contains the verb in the subjunctive and is often introduced by *que.*

-it can also be used alone in idiomatic expressions:

Sauve qui peut!

Vive la République!

Soit!

in third person singular or plural, preceded by *que* it is used as a command:

Que tout le monde se taise!

Le silence va parler.

-there are four conditions that call for the use of the subjunctive:

volition   emotion

unreality   doubt and **denial**

Uses of the subjunctive:

-after some conjunctions and expressions of

-concession:

bien que	*quoique*
though	although
où que	*que... ou non*
wherever	whether.. or not
quel que	*qui que*
whatever	whoever

-purpose:

afin que	pour que
in order that	so that

-fear:

de crainte que	de peur que
for fear that	for fear that

-restriction:

à moins que	à condition que
unless	on condition that
pourvu que	avant que
provided that	before
jusqu'à ce que	en attendant que
until	while, until
sans que	
without	

-after impersonal expressions:

il est bon que	it is good that
il est désirable que	it is desirable that
il est dommage que	it is a pity that
il est douteux que	it is doubtful that
il est étonnant que	it is astonishing that
il faut que	it is necessary that
il est important que	it is important that
il est temps que	it is time that
il est nécessaire que	it is necessary that

il est obligatoire que	it is obligatory that
il est utile/inutile que	it is useful/unuseful that
il est préférable que	it is preferable that
il vaut mieux que	it is better that

-after volition verbs*:

aimer que	conseiller que
to like that	to advise that
demander que	défendre que
to ask that	to forbid that
désirer que	empêcher que
to desire that	to prevent that
exiger que	recommander que
to demand that	to recommend that
suggérer que	vouloir que
to suggest that	to want that

*Je te suggère que tu **te lèves** tôt.*

-after emotion expressions*: joy, regret, sorrow, fear, surprise: to be . . .   that

être heureux que	happy
être content que	happy
être ravi que	delighted
être désolé que	sorry
être malheureux que	unhappy
être triste que	sad
être furieux que	furious
être étonné que	astonished

être surpris que   surprised

avoir peur que   afraid

craindre que   fear

regretter que   be sorry

    *On regrette qu'elle **parte**.*

*use the subjunctive if the subject in the main and in the subordinate clause is different. If there is no subject change, use the indicative.

    ***Je** voudrais que **vous** finissiez votre roman.*

    ***Il** est content que **sa mère** soit revenue.*

    ***Il** voudrait finir son roman.*

    ***Je** suis contente de pouvoir partir.*

douter que	*nier que*
to doubt that	to deny that
n'être pas sûr que	*ne pas penser que*
not to be sure that	not to think that
n'être pas certain que	*n'être pas clair que*
not to be certain that	not to be clear that

Je ne crois pas   *qu'il **vienne.***

Je ne suis pas sûr   ”

Je ne pense pas   ”

Je ne suis pas certain   ”

but

Je suis sûr   *qu'il **viendra**.*

Je pense   ”

Je crois   ”

Je suis certain   ”

Present subjunctive:

-it is formed with the **third person plural of the present indicative minus *-ent* + the endings**

    (ils) parlent ⇒ *parl* + the following endings

singular	je	stem	+	-e
	tu	stem	+	-es
	il/elle	stem	+	-e
plural	nous	stem	+	-ions
	vous	stem	+	-iez
	ils/elles	stem	+	-ent

All the verbs except ***être*** and ***avoir*** have the same endings.

	avoir	**être**
que	j'aie	je sois
que	tu aies	tu sois
qu'	il ait	il soit
qu'	elle ait	elle soit
que	nous ayons	nous soyons
que	vous ayez	vous soyez
qu'	ils aient	ils soient
qu'	elles aient	elles soient

-it is used when the actions in both clauses take place simultaneously or, to indicate posteriority, when the action in the subordinate clause takes place after the action or idea in the main clause.

-the verb of the main clause can be in the present, past, future or conditional:

Je suis content que tu sois ici.   (now)

J'étais content que tu sois ici.   (yesterday)

Je serai content que tu sois ici.   (tomorrow)

Je serais content que tu sois ici. (one day)

Je ne suis pas sûr qu'ils réussissent au prochain examen.

Verbs with irregular stems:

savoir (to know)   → **sach** + subj. ends

pouvoir (to be able to do) → **puiss** + subj. ends

faire (to do/make)   → **fass** + subj. ends

pleuvoir (to rain)   → *qu'il pleuve*

falloir (to be necessary) → *qu'il faille*

valoir (to be worth)   → *qu'il vaille*

Verbs with two different irregular stems

-**one for** the singular and the third plural forms.

-**the second for** *nous, vous.*

aller (to go)	→ *aill*	+ subj endings
	→ *all*	+ subj endings
boire (to drink)	→ *boi*	+ subj endings
	→ *buv*	+ subj endings
croire (to believe)	→ *croi*	+ subj endings
	→ *croy*	+ subj endings
devoir (to owe)	→ *doiv*	+ subj endings
	→ *dev*	+ subj endings
prendre (to take)	→ *prenn*	+ subj endings
	→ *pren*	+ subj endings
recevoir (to receive)	→ *reçoiv*	+ subj endings
	→ *recev*	+ subj endings
tenir (to have)	→ *tienn*	+ subj endings
	→ *ten*	+ subj endings
valoir (to be worth)	→ *vaill*	+ subj endings
	→ *val*	+ subj endings
venir (to come)	→ *vienn*	+ subj endings
	→ *ven*	+ subj endings
voir (to see)	→ *voi*	+ subj endings
	→ *voy*	+ subj endings
vouloir (to want)	→ *veuill*	+ subj endings
	→ *voul*	+ subj endings

-it is used when the action or idea expressed in the subordinate clause took place or needed to take place before the action or the idea in the main clause.

-the verb in the main clause can be in present, past, future or conditional:

*Je suis contente que tu **aies réussi** à l'examen.*

*Il aurait fallu qu'il **soit parti** avant trois heures.*

-the **imperfect subjunctive** is formed by dropping the ending of the passé simple and adding the imperfect subj. endings

-er verbs	que je	-asse
	que tu	-asses
	qu' il	
	qu' elle	-ât
	que nous	-assions
	que vous	-assiez
	qu'ils	
	qu'elles	-assent
-ir verbs	que je	-isse
	que tu	-isses
	qu'il	
	qu'elle	-ît
	que nous	-issions
	que vous	-issiez
	qu'ils	
	qu'elles	-issent
-re verbs	que je	-usse
	que tu	-usses
	qu'il	
	qu'elle	-ût
	que nous	-ussions
	que vous	-ussiez
	qu'ils	
	qu'elles	-ussent

The **pluperfect subjunctive** is formed with the imperfect subjunctive of the auxiliary verb + the past participle.

```
imp. subj. avoir    +    past part
que j'eusse         +
que tu eusses       +
qu'il
qu'elle eût         +
que nous eussions   +
que vous eussiez    +
qu'ils
qu'elles eussent    +

imp. subj. être     +    past part
que je fusse        +
que tu fusses       +
qu'il
qu'elle fût         +
que nous fussions   +
que vous fussiez    +
qu'ils
qu'elles fussent    +
```

	Chart X.	Subjunctive or indicative?	
Subjunctive	**use** ←	SUBJUNCTIVE OR INDICATIVE? ⇒ **use**	**Indicative**
X	← **Doubt**: *douter, être probable,* **ne pas** *croire,* **ne pas** *penser*		
	but:	*croire, penser* imply certainty ⇒	X
X	← **request**: *prier, supplier, demander...* **que**		
	⇒	**but:** *prier, supplier, demander...* **de**	X
X	← **willing**: *aimer, désirer, insister à, préférer, permettre, vouloir, exiger, ordonner, défendre, empêcher, recommander, suggérer, conseiller ...* **que**		
	but: *ordonner, défendre, empêcher, recommander, suggérer, permettre, conseiller ...* **de** ⇒		X
X	← **emotion**: *être... heureux que, ravis que, désolé que, malheureux que, triste que, furieux que, étonné que, surpris que* & *craindre, regretter que*		
	but:	if there is no change of subject ⇒	X
X	← **with impersonal expressions**: *il est... bon que, désirable que, dommage que, douteux que, étonnant que, important que, temps que, nécessaire que, obligatoire que, utile/inutile que, préférable que* & *il faut/vaut mieux que*		
	but: when the subject is neither expressed nor implied use **de + infinitive** -with impersonal expressions that express a certainty: *C'est... certain, vrai, sûr... que* ⇒		X
X	← **with** *pourvu que* before the verb to express doubt or uncertainty		
X	←**in adverb clauses**, to relate an event or action that is indef. or uncert.: *pour que, afin que, sans que, à moins que, à condition que, avant que, pourvu que, de peur que*		
	after: *malgré que, lorsque, pendant que, après que, jusqu'à ce que, dès que* to introduce forthcoming events, hypothetical actions or something that has not yet occurred, or to refer to an action that has happened, is happening or habitually happens ⇒		X
X	← **in adjective clauses**: if the antecedent is indefinite, non existent, hypothetical or negative.		
	but:	if it is definite, specific or known to exist ⇒	X
X	**after**: *admettre, comprendre, dire, écrire, entendre, expliquer, se plaindre, prétendre, téléphoner, être d'avis...* ← **appreciation**: judgement or opinion statement ⇒		X

Chart XI.   Patterns of conjugation of -er, -ir, -re regular verbs.

			Present		Passé composé		Imperfect	
					[pres. *avoir* or *être* + past participle:]		**nous** form pres. ind.	
		inf.minus	+	inf.minus	+	minus	+
je	**er**	- er	e	- er	é	- ons	ais
tu			es		é		ais
il/elle			e		é		ait
nous			ons		é		ions
vous			ez		é		iez
ils/elles			ent		é		aient
je	**ir**	**- ir**	**is**	**- ir**	**i**	**- ons**	**ais**
tu			**is**		**i**		**ais**
il/elle			**it**		**i**		**ait**
nous			**issons**		**i**		**ions**
vous			**issez**		**i**		**iez**
ils/elles			**issent**		**i**		**aient**
je	**er**	- re	s	- re	u	- ons	ais
tu			s		u		ais
il/elle			-		u		ait
nous			ons		u		ions
vous			ez		u		iez
ils/elles			ent		u		aient

Chart XI. . . .

			Future		Conditional		Subjunctive	
							ils form present indicative minus **ent** +	
			infinitive +		infinitive +			
je	**er**	infin.	ai	infin.	ais	- ent	e
tu			as		ais		es
il/elle			a		ait		e
nous			ons		ions		ions
vous			ez		iez		iez
ils/elles			ont		aient		ent
je	**ir**	**infin.**	**ai**	**infin.**	**ais**	**- ent**	**e**
tu			**as**		**ais**		**es**
il/elle			**a**		**ait**		**e**
nous			**ons**		**ions**		**ions**
vous			**ez**		**iez**		**iez**
ils/elles			**ont**		**aient**		**ent**
je	**er**	inf - e	ai	infin.	ais	-ent	e
tu			as		ais		es
il/elle			a		ait		e
nous			ons		ions		ions
vous			ez		iez		iez
ils/elles			ont		aient		ent

Imperative: it is a mood that expresses commands, requests or directions.

-the *tu, vous* and *nous* forms of the present indicative without the subject pronoun are used to form the imperative.

-irregular verbs in the imperative:

être (to be)	**avoir** (to have)
sois	aie
soyons	ayons
soyez	ayez
savoir (to know)	**vouloir** (to want)
sache	veuille
sachons	veuillons
sachez	veuillez *polite form

-in the negative form *ne* (*n'* in front of a vowel or mute h) precedes the verb and **pas** follows it:

*N'ayez **pas** peur.*

-the verbs with irregular stem in the present are irregular in the imperative.

-the -**er** ending verbs and the verbs *aller, offrir, souffrir, ouvrir, couvrir, découvrir* et *récouvrir,* drop the -*s* of the *tu* form in the

imperative except in front of *y* and *en*:

Va te coucher! Vas-y!

-in the affirmative form of the imperative the object pronouns follow the verb attached to it by a hyphen. (*me* ⇒ *moi* and *te* ⇒ *toi*)

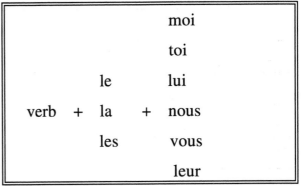

*Donnez-**le** moi!*

-in a negative command the object pronoun precedes the verb:

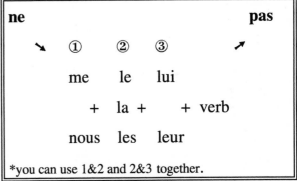

*Ne **me le** donnez pas!*

*Ne **le lui** donne pas!*

- *y* and *en* precede directly the verb:

*Ne m'**en** parle pas!   N'**y** pense plus!*

Español	English	Français
Presente: *amo*	**Present:** *I love*	**Présent:** *j'aime*
Presente progresivo: presente de *estar*+part. pres. *estoy amando*	**Present progressive:** present of *to be* +ing form *I'm loving*	**Présent progressif:** *je suis en train de* +infinitif *je suis en train d'aimer*
Pretérito perfecto: presente de *haber*+part. pas. *he amado*	**Present perfect:** *have/has* + past part. *I have loved*	**Passé composé:** prés. *être* ou *avoir*+part. passé *j'ai aimé*
Pretérito indefinido: *amé*	**Past or preterite:** *I loved*	**Passé simple:** *j'aimai*
Pasado progresivo: imp. de *estar* + part presente *estaba amando*	**Past progressive:** *was/were* + ing form *I was loving*	**Passé progressif:** J'étais en train de + infinitif *J'étais en train d'aimer*
Pretérito anterior: pret.indef. de *haber*+part. pas. *hube amado*	**Past perfect:** *had* + past part. *I had loved*	**Passé antérieur:** passé simple *avoir* ou *être* + part. passé *J'eus aimé*
Imperfecto: *amaba*	**Imperfect:** *I used to love*	**Imparfait:** *J'aimais*
Pluscuamperfecto: imper.de *haber*+part. pasado *había amado*	**Plusperfect:** corresponds to the past perfect: *I had loved*	**Plus-que-parfait:** imparfait d'*avoir* ou *être* + part. passé *j'avais aimé*
Futuro: *amaré*	**Future:** *I shall love*	**Futur:** *J'aimerai*
Futuro inmediato: presente de *ir* + *a* + infinitivo *Voy a amar*	**Near future:** *to be going* + inf. *I'm going to love*	**Futur immédiat/proche:** présent d'*aller* + inf. *Je vais aimer*
Futuro perfecto: futuro de *haber*+part. pasado *habré amado*	**Future perfect:** *shall/will have* + past. part. *I will have loved*	**Futur antérieur:** futur *avoir* ou *être*+part. passé *j'aurai aimé*

Futuro progresivo: *habremos estado+* part. pres. *habremos estado amando*	**Future progressive:** *shall/will have been+*present part. *I will have been loving*	**Futur progressif:** *aurions été + en train de...* *aurions été en train d'aimer*
Condicional: presente infinitivo+terminaciones [ía/ías/ía / íamos/íais/ían] *amaría*	**Conditional: present** *would* + present tense *would love*	**Conditionnel: présent** infinitif + terminaisons [ais/ais/ait / ions/iez/aient] *j'aimerais*
Condicional: pasado condicional presente de *haber* + part. pasado *habría amado*	**Conditional: perfect** *would+have+* past participle *would have loved*	**Conditionnel: passé** conditionnel présent d'*avoir* ou *être* + part. passé *j'aurais aimé*
Subjuntivo: presente elimine la *o* de la primera pers. sing. del presente del indicativo+ las terminaciones [-ar: e/es/e / emos/éis/en -er/-ir:a/as/a / amos/áis/an] *que yo ame*	**Subjunctive: present** present minus -*s* of the third person sing. *that I love*	**Subjonctif: présent** radical de la 3ème p.plurielle de l'ind. prés + terminaisons [e/es/e / ions/iez/ent] *que j'aime*
Subjuntivo: imperfecto tercera pers. pl. del pretérito indef. menos ***ron*** +termin. [ra/ras/ra / ramos/rais/ran] *amara*	**Subjunctive: imperfect** corresponds to past tense indicative. *that I loved*	**Subjonctif: imparfait** passé simple de l'indicatif + terminaisons [sse/sses/ ^t / ssions/ssiez/ssent] *que j'aimasse*
Subj.: pretérito perfecto presente del subj. de *haber* + part. pasado *haya amado*	**Subj.: present perfect** corresponds to present perfect indicative. *that I have loved*	**Subjonctif: passé** présent du subj d'*avoir* ou *être* + part.passé *que j'aie aimé*
Subj.: pluscuamperfecto imperfecto del subj. de *haber* + part. pasado *hubiera amado*	**Subj.: plusperfect** or **past perfect** corresponds to past perfect indicative *that I had loved*	**Subjonctif: plus-que-parfait** imparfait du subj d'*avoir* ou *être* + part. passé *que j'eusse aimé*

Imperativo:(formal) raíz de la primera pers. sing. del pres. del ind. + *e* [verbos-ar] o *a* [verbos er/ir] *ame* **Imperativo:**(informal) afirmativo es igual a la 3a per. sing. del presente indicativo *ama* negativo es igual a la 2a per. sing. del presente subjuntivo	**Imperative:** infinitive minus *to*	**Impératif:** les formes verbales sont celles de la deuxième personne [sing. et plur.] et la première du pluriel du présent indicatif sans le pronom sujet. Les verbes dont la 2ème personne du singulier est terminée par **-es** éliminent le *s* final, sauf quand l'impératif est suivi des pronoms *en* et *y*.
no ames	*love!*	*aime! aimez! aimons!*

Idiom expressions with verbs.

With être: are used to express conditions or feelings.

-to modify them use the adverb *très*.

-never use *beaucoup*.

a form of être + an adjective:

Je suis fatigué/e	I am tired
heureux/euse	happy
triste	sad
malade	sick
ennuyé/e	bored
occupé/e	busy
préoccupé/e	worried
énervé/e	nervous
content/e	happy
prêt/e	ready
fou/folle	crazy
sûr/e	sure
vivant/e	alive
mort/e	dead

Common expressions with être.

être d'accord	to agree with

***être en train de* + infinitive**: it indicates an action in progress.

Je suis en train de manger.	I'm eating.
. . . *jouer*	I'm playing.
. . . *étudier*	I'm studying

être à l'heure	to be on time
en retard	late
en avance	early
Quelle heure est-il?	What time is it?
Il est une heure.	It is one o'clock.

Idiom expressions with avoir:

-a form of *avoir* + a noun:

J'ai faim.	I am hungry.
soif	thirsty
froid	cold
chaud	hot
sommeil	sleepy
peur	afraid

de la chance	lucky		*du soleil*	sunny
raison	right		*jour*	daylight
tort	wrong		*nuit*	dark
... ans	..... years old		*sec*	dry
honte	ashamed		*humide*	humid
			bon	nice
			Il fait de l'orage.	stormy
			Il se fait tard.	It is getting late.

Common expressions with avoir:

avoir besoin de	to need
envie de	to wish
l'habitude de	to have the habit
l'intention de	to have the intention
l'âge de	to have the age of

Common expressions with faire:

Ça fait bien!	It looks good.
Ça fait mal!	It hurts!
Ça fait du bien.	It's good.
Ça fait du mal.	It's bad.
Ça ne fait rien.	It doesn't matter.
C'est bien fait!	Serves them right!

Idiom expressions with faire:

-*faire* with expressions of time and weather:

Il fait beau.	The weather is fine.
mauvais	is bad
chaud	it is hot
frais	cool
froid	cold
doux	mild
du vent	windy

Mener - Porter

-*mener* and its compounds: *amener, ramener, emmener, remmener* are used for persons, animals or objects able to move by themselves. (*Jean, le chat, une voiture*).

-*porter* and its compounds: *apporter, rapporter, emporter remporter* are used in general for objects you need to move.

-*mener* can be translated by **to lead**.
-*porter* can be translated by **to carry**.

-*amener*: *conduire quelqu'un à un endroit ou avec soi*; can be translated by **to bring** (to a different place from the here of the speaker).

Mes parents m'amenaient chez mon cousin pour les vacances, puis ils rentraient à Paris.

-*ramener* can be translated by **to bring back**.

Amenez votre copine à la fête mais souvenez-vous, si vous prenez plus de trois verres, demandez à un ami de vous ramener chez vous. C'est plus sûr.

-*emmener*: can be translated by **to take along** (from the here of the speaker to a different place).

Mes parents aimaient nous emmener avec eux en vacances en Italie.

Pierre, emmenez-moi dîner à la Tour d'argent ce soir.

-*remmener* can be translated by **to take back** (to the place from where you took it).

Amenez l'enfant à l'école, puis remmenez-le chez lui.

-*apporter* can be translated by **to bring**.
-*rapporter* can be translated by **to bring back**.

-*emporter* can be translated by **to take along**.
-*remporter* can be translated by **to take back**.

Apportez vos fiches à la classe, mais n'oubliez pas de les remporter à la fin du cours.

Savoir - Connaître:

Savoir: means to know facts, numbers or other specific information thoroughly, by heart or from learning.

Je sais qui c'est l'assassin.

-*savoir* + infinitive: means to know how to do something.

Je sais conduire.

-it may be used with or without a direct object.

Je sais la leçon par coeur.

-it may be followed by a clause beginning with *que, pourquoi, quand,* etc...

Je sais que tu sais.

Connaître means to know a person in the sense of to be familiar with, to meet or to be acquainted with things, places or situations as a result of an experience.

Je connais l'assassin, monsieur le juge, c'est mon mari.

Connaître means to know...

-*connaître* must be followed by a direct object.

-it can not be followed by a *que* clause.

connaître		
singular	je	connais
	tu	connais
	il/elle	connaît
plural	nous	connaissons
	vous	connaissez
	ils/elles	connaissent

savoir		
singular	je	sais
	tu	sais
	il/elle	sait
plural	nous	savons
	vous	savez
	ils/elles	savent

Savoir - Pouvoir

Note also the distinction between *savoir* and *pouvoir*.

-*savoir* + **infinitive** means to know how to do something

-*pouvoir* + **infinitive** means to be able to do something.

-if the verb indicates mental ability *savoir* is used

Savez-vous lire?

Do you know how to read?

-if the verb expresses physical ability, *pouvoir* is used.

Pouvez-vous courir?

Can you run?

	pouvoir	
singular	je	peux
	tu	peux
	il/elle	peut
plural	nous	pouvons
	vous	pouvez
	ils/elles	peuvent

> **Prepositions**: they are invariable connecting words placed before a substantive that indicate the relation of that substantive to the verb, an adjective or another substantive.

Of place:

-they are used to situate things and people in the space.

à: inside/at/to

chez: at the house/place of

contre: against

en: in/at/into

dans	≠	*hors de*
inside/within	≠	outside/out of
devant	≠	*derrière*
in front of	≠	behind
sous	≠	*sur*
under	≠	on
près de	≠	*loin de*
near	≠	far from
à droite	≠	*à gauche*
on the right	≠	on the left
en haut de	≠	*en bas de*
over	≠	under

en face de: across from/facing

a côté de: beside/next to

de l'autre côté de: on the other side of

le long de: along

au-dessous de	≠	*au-dessus de*
beneath	≠	over

au milieu de: in the middle of

entre: between

parmi: among

d'entre: among

autour de: around

parmi, used in front of a plural noun, denotes more than two persons or objects:

> *Elle était **parmi** la foule.*

entre is used when you have only two persons or objects:

> *Il était **entre** les deux filles.*

d'entre is used in front of a stressed pronoun:

> *Dix **d'entre** eux ont passé l'examen.*

Of time:

-they are used to indicate relations of time.

après	after
avant	before
dès	from... on
depuis	since
pendant	during
aux environs de	about
en début de	at the beginning of
en fin de	at the end of
au milieu de	in the middle of
au moment de	at the time of
entre	between

pour (for) + time expression to indicate a period of time to be spent:

*Elle ira à Paris **pour** deux mois.*

dans + time expression to indicate the time will elapse before something begins:

***Dans** un mois il sera célèbre.*

-*dans* + place: *dans le salon*
dans l'armoire   dans la chambre

The prepositions *à* and *de* introduce several complements:

-**indirect objects**:

*Tu parles **à** ta femme.*

-**circunstances**:

*Nous irons **à** la campagne.*

*Nous venons **de** la campagne.*

-**noun or adjective complements**:

*Les livres **de** Gustavo sont pleins **d'**images poétiques.*

*Une barbe **à** papa est difficile **à** manger.*

-verbs followed by the preposition *à* + infinitive:

s'amuser to have fun	*apprendre* to learn	*arriver* to arrive
chercher to look for	*continuer* to continue	*commencer* to begin
se décider to decide	*s'habituer* to get used to	*hésiter* to hesitate
se mettre to put/place oneself	*parvenir* to succeed/ attain	*penser* to think
réussir to succeed	*tenir* to have/possess	

. . . à + infinitive

-verbs followed by the preposition *de* + **infinitive**:

accepter to accept	*arrêter* to stop	*avoir besoin* to need
avoir envie to want	*avoir peur* to be afraid	*cesser* to cease
choisir to choose	*craindre* to be afraid	*décider* to decide
se dépêcher to hurry	*essayer* to try	*éviter* to avoid
faire to do/make	*exprimer* to express	*finir* to finish
oublier to forget	*refuser* to refuse	*regretter* to regret
tâcher to spot/stain	*commencer* to begin	*continuer* to continue

. . . *de* + **infinitive**

-the other prepositions are used to introduce the circunstances of the events.:

place *devant*

time *après*

goals *pour*

manner *avec* + adjective

means *avec/sans* + noun

en: (in/at) is used **to** indicate:

place: *en France*

time: *en hiver*

material: *en bois*

means of transport: *en voiture*

à cause de ≠ malgré

because of ≠ in spite of

à cause de indicates reason and is followed by a noun or pronoun, *malgré* indicates opposition:

A ***cause de*** *mon travail j' ai été reconnue au niveau national.*

Malgré *mon travail j'ai été licenciée.*

voici ≠ voilà

voir ci   voir là

they are relative prepositions used to designate a person or thing relatively near (*-ci*) or relatively far (*-là*) from the speaker:

Voici mes fleurs

voici mes rêves

voici ma vie.

Voilà mes fleurs qui meurent

voilà mes rêves qui s'évanouissent

voilà ma vie qui disparaît.

Me voilà retournant à la vie entre vos mains sacrées.

Gustavo

Chart XIII.

à, en and *dans* with geographic names:

cities	à		
countries continents masculine	à	beginning in vowel: en	
feminine		en	
masc. plural	aux		
regions:feminine & masculine beginning in vowel		en	
regions: +article + masculine beginning in consonant			dans
islands: without article	à		
islands: with article		en	

Pour - Par

Pour: expresses destination for a specific person, thing or organization. (for)

*Ces fleurs sont **pour** toi.*

-***pour***: in the direction of, toward:

*Hier ils sont partis **pour** la France.*

-***pour*** replaces **pendant** after the verbs of motion or with future actions (for):

*J'irai à Paris **pour** deux mois.*

-***pour*** + infinitive means in order to:

*Je suis venu **pour** te dire au revoir.*

***Pour** commencer je voudrais vous parler de Sans détour.*

***Pour** finir je vous demande d'étudier les fiches avec soin.*

-***pour que*** expresses a goal (so that):

*Je vous enseigne **pour que** vous puissiez réussir.*

-considering, compared with others, in relation to others or to make judgements in one's opinion:

***Pour** lui rien n'est difficile.*

***Pour** un étranger, il parle bien le français.*

-***pour***: in the employ of:

*Il travaille **pour** le gouvernement.*

-***pour***: by or for, when it expresses a deadline:

*J'ai besoin du compte rendu **pour** mardi prochain, svp.*

Par: (through/by) **is used to indicate motion through or by a place.**

*Il a passé **par** Paris.*

*Nous sommes entrés **par** la porte principale.*

-***par*** is used to express the agent in a passive voice:

*Ce livre a été écrit **par** un maître.*

-after commencer and finir use ***par*** + infinitive:

*J'ai fini **par** comprendre, s'écria Juliette.*

-***par*** + noun to express frecuency or amount per unit of time:

*Je vais en France deux fois **par** an.*

*Je gagne cinquante dollars **par** jour.*

but:

Je gagne dix dollars de l'heure. (per hour)

Je roulais à 90 kilomètres à l'heure. (per hour)

> **Coordinating conjunctions**: they connect two words, parts of a sentence, groups of words or propositions.

et and	*mais* but	*ou/ou bien* or
ni nor	*ainsi/donc/en conséquence* so	*que* that, which, who

-they join two elements of equal valeu:

-a word to another word:

*fraises **et** chocolat*

strawberries **and** chocolate

-a phrase to another phrase without dependance:

*Tu peux te garer au garage **ou** devant la maison.*

You may park in the garage **or** in front of the house.

-a clause dependent to another dependent clause:

*Je suis allé au théâtre **mais** je suis arrivé trop tard.*

I went to the theater **but** I arrived too late.

- an independent clause to another independent clause:

*Il aime avoir du pognon **mais** il hait travailler.*

He likes to make money **but** he hates to work.

> **Conjunctions of time**: they express previousness, simultaneity or posteriority

quand when	*avant que* before	*après que* after
pendant que while	**aussitôt que* as soon as	**dès que* as soon as
jusqu'à ce que until		**lorsque /quand* when

*after these conjunctions the future tense is used whenever there's a future connotation.

Conjunctions of purpose: they link an independent clause to a dependent clause.

à moins que unless	*pourvu que* provided	*à condition que* provided that
sans que without	*pour que* so, in order to	*afin que* in order that
pour que so that	*tant que* as long as	*au cas où* in case

Subordinating or adverbial conjunctions: they link a subordinate proposition to the main clause.

après que after	*quoique* although	*comme* as
tant que as long as	*dès que* as soon as	*parce que* because
maintenant now	*afin que* in order that	*si* if
ainsi que so that	*que* than	*pendant* while
comme si as if	*avant que* before	*depuis* since
au moins unless que	*jusqu'à* until	*quand* when
	où where	

Une fois le travail fini nous irons au cinéma.

After we finish the work we will go to the movies.

Malgré que je m'intérese à ses romans je n'assisterai pas à sa conférence ce soir.

Although I'm usually interested in his novels, I'd rather not go to his conference tonight.

Tant qu'il écrira je serai tranquille.

As long as he writes I will be in peace.

S.v.p. traitez-moi comme si j'étais votre frère, dit Caïn.

Please, treat me **as if** I were your brother, said Cain.

Parce que malade je ne peux pas aller au théâtre.

Because I'm sick, I cannot go to the theater.

Adversative conjunctions: they express antithesis or opposition.

mais but	*sino* on the contrary, rather
sino que but instead	*cependant* nevertheless

ACCENTS AND DIACRITICS.

The written accent marks in French are three:

accent aigu: é
accent grave: à, è, ù
accent circonflexe: â, ê, î, ô, û

the **accent aigu** it is only used on the vowel *e* which is then pronounced [e] instead of [ə]

téléphone   doré parlé Américain chanté

the **accent grave**:

-on the vowel *e* it changes its pronunciation to [ɛ]

père   mère   célèbre   ténèbres

we can find it most of all in the ending *è* + consonant + mute *e*.

-on the vowels *à* or *ù* it is used to distinguish homonyms.

il a	*à*
(he has)	(preposition)
ou	*où*
(or)	(where)

la	*là*
(fem.def.art.)	(adverb)

the **accent circonflexe**: it is used to show that the pronunciation of that vowel is longer than without it.

pâte   tête   connaît

-to distinguish homonyms:

cote	*côte*
(rating, popularity)	(rib, coast)
du	*dû*
(partitive art.)	(past part.)
sur	sûr
(on)	(sure)
mur	*mûre*
(wall)	(ripe)

-the **cédille** is placed under a *c* [ç] in front of the vowels *a, o* or *u* to indicate that it is pronounced *s*.

ça   français   François

the **tréma**: *ë, ï, ü* is placed on the second vowel of a group to indicate that the vowel before is pronounced separately.

naïf   Noël   aiguë   Saül

STRESSING:

the tonic of a word in French goes usually on the last vowel pronounced.

chemin   *journal*   *émotion*

but

a mute *e* at the end of a word, even if it is pronounced is never stressed.*

parle   *latitude*

*note: the endings *e* and *es* of polysyllables as well as the **ent** ending of third person plural verbs are mute.

porte   *portes*   *portent*

SYLLABICATION.

All the French words are divided into as many syllables as it has vowel sounds.

How to divide into syllables:

1.- a consonant and a vowel

consonnat   vowel ÷

divide after the vowel

pe ti te   *gé né ral*   *mi di*

ch, ph are considered single consonants

che mi se   *Chi li*   *té lé pho ne*   *pho to*

2.- two consonants:

consonant   ÷   consonant

divide between the consonants

ac teur   *ar ti cle*   *gros se*   *pro gram me*
but

consonant   +   l   or   r   ÷

are indivisible

a près   *ai gle*   *in vi si ble*

3.- three consonants:

```
consonant   consonant   ÷   consonant
```

divide before the last consonant

ins ti tu tion

but

```
consonant   ÷   consonant + l or r
```

divide after the first consonant

com pli ment   com pren dre

4.- four consonants:

```
cons. cons.    ÷    cons.  cons
```

divide in the middle

cons trui re   ins truc teur

Single syllables formed by the combination of two or three vowels.

ai	*lait*
au	*au to*
eau	*beau*
ei	*vei ne*
eu	*pleu reur*
eui	*é cu reuil*

oei	*oeil*
oeu	*oeu vre*
oi	*voi là*
oie	*oie*
ou	*cou rir*
oui	*Louis*
ui	*cuis son*

Division of words at the end of a line.

-the syllabic division is usually used:

cons-cience   cons-pirer

-never divide a word sending to the next line a mute syllable, and the division must leave at least two letters at the end of a line.

✗ *publi-que   mélan-ge*

√ *pu-blique   mé-lange*

-neither divide **before or after** an *x* or a *y* between two vowels

✗ *infle-x-ible   deu-x-ième   vo-y-eur*

but

the division between those letters is possible whenever they are followed by a consonant

√ *tex-ture   pay-sage   pay-san*

-a set of initials is never divided

✗ *O.-N.U*

√ *O.N.U.   O.E.A.   O.T.A.N.   P.T.T.*

-do not divide the initials from the name that follows

✗ *Mme.-Pernaud   M.-Proust*

√ *Mme. Pernaud   M. Proust*

-do not divide a name compound of letters and numbers

✗ *Paul -VI   Léon -XIII   Vème-République*

√ *Paul VI   Léon XIII   Vème République*

- do not divide the dates

✗ *le 14 -juillet   le 14 juillet -1789*

√ *le 14 juillet   le 14 juillet 1789*

The liaison:

-pronunciation of the usually silent final consonant of a word when followed by a word beginning with a vowel.

s, x, t, d, r, p, g, f and *n* generally mute, in liaison they are pronounced as follows:

s x z	[z]	*les_amis, aux_armes allez_y*
t, d	[t]	*petit_enfant, grand_enfant*
r	[r]	*le premier_arrivé*
p	[p]	*trop_aimable*
g	[g]	*long_attente*
f	[v]	*neuf_ans*
n	[n]	*bon_ami*

mandatory liaisons:

-between the definite and indefinite articles, the demonstrative and possessive adjectives, interrogative and exclamation words **and a noun**:

les_amis   un_arbre

aux_armes   ces_enfants

-between the definite and indefinite articles, the demonstrative and possessive adjectives, interrogative and exclamation words **and an adjective or a noun**:

mes_anciens_amis

-between one or two pronouns and a verb:

Ils_en_ont   Allez-y!

-after an adverb or a monosyllabic preposition and after *après*:

bien_aimable

très_amical

-after *quand* et *dont*

quand_on publiera mon livre...

forbidden liaisons:

- after a singular noun:

-after *et*

- in front of an aspirate *h*

-in front of *onze* and *oui*

- after: *comment, quand* and *combien*

except: *comment_-allez-vous?*

-in plural compound nouns:

salles   à manger

-in front of [j] or [w] in foreign nouns

-between *ils, elles* or *on* and an infinitive or past participle. *Vont-ils   arriver?*

présent	passé composé	imparfait	futur	conditionnel	pr. subjonctif

accepter: to accept

présent	passé composé	imparfait	futur	conditionnel	pr. subjonctif
accepte	ai accepté	acceptais	accepterai	accepterais	accepte
acceptes	as accepté	acceptais	accepteras	accepterais	acceptes
accepte	a accepté	acceptait	acceptera	accepterait	accepte
acceptons	avons accepté	acceptions	accepterons	accepterions	acceptions
acceptez	avez accepté	acceptiez	accepterez	accepteriez	acceptiez
acceptent	ont accepté	acceptaient	accepteront	accepteraient	acceptent

impératif: accepte acceptons acceptez

accorder: to accord

présent	passé composé	imparfait	futur	conditionnel	pr. subjonctif
accorde	ai accordé	accordais	accorderai	accorderais	accorde
accordes	as accordé	accordais	accorderas	accorderais	accordes
accorde	a accordé	accordait	accordera	accorderait	accorde
accordons	avons accordé	accordions	accorderons	accorderions	accordions
accordez	avez accordé	accordiez	accorderez	accorderiez	accordiez
accordent	ont accordé	accordaient	accorderont	accorderaient	accordent

impératif: accorde accordons accordez

accueillir: to welcome/greet

présent	passé composé	imparfait	futur	conditionnel	pr. subjonctif
accueille	ai accueilli	accueillais	accueillerai	accueillerais	accueille
accueilles	as accueilli	accueillais	accueilleras	accueillerais	accueilles
accueille	a accueilli	accueillait	accueillera	accueillerait	accueille
accueillons	avons accueilli	accueillions	accueillerons	accueillerions	accueillions
accueillez	avez accueilli	accueilliez	accueillerez	accueilleriez	accueilliez
accueillent	ont accueilli	accueillaient	accueilleront	accueilleraient	accueillent

impératif: accueille accueillons accueillez

présent	passé composé	imparfait	futur	conditionnel	pr. subjonctif

acheter: to buy

achète	ai acheté	achetais	achèterai	achèterais	achète
achètes	as acheté	achetais	achèteras	achèterais	achètes
achète	a acheté	achetait	achètera	achèterait	achète
achetons	avons acheté	achetions	achèterons	achèterions	achetions
achetez	avez acheté	achetiez	achèterez	achèteriez	achetiez
achètent	ont acheté	achetaient	achèteront	achèteraient	achètent

impératif: achète achetons achetez

admettre: to admit

admets	ai admis	admettais	admettrai	admettrais	admette
admets	as admis	admettais	admettras	admettrais	admettes
admet	a admis	admettait	admettra	admettrait	admettte
admettons	avons admis	admettions	admettrons	admettrions	admettions
admettez	avez admis	admettiez	admettrez	admettriez	admettiez
admettent	ont admis	admettaient	admettront	admettraient	admetttent

impératif: admets admettons admettez

aider: to help

aide	ai aidé	aidais	aiderai	aiderais	aide
aides	as aidé	aidais	aideras	aiderais	aides
aide	a aidé	aidait	aidera	aiderait	aide
aidons	avons aidé	aidions	aiderons	aiderions	aidions
aidez	avez aidé	aidiez	aiderez	aideriez	aidiez
aident	ont aidé	aidaient	aideront	aideraient	aident

impératif: aide aidons aidez

	présent	passé composé	imparfait	futur	conditionnel	pr. subjonctif

aimer: to love

présent	passé composé	imparfait	futur	conditionnel	pr. subjonctif
aime	ai aimé	aimais	aimerai	aimerais	aime
aimes	as aimé	aimais	aimeras	aimerais	aimes
aime	a aimé	aimait	aimera	aimerait	aime
aimons	avons aimé	aimions	aimerons	aimerions	aimions
aimez	avez aimé	aimiez	aimerez	aimeriez	aimiez
aiment	ont aimé	aimaient	aimeront	aimeraient	aiment

impératif: aime aimons aimez

aller: to go

présent	passé composé	imparfait	futur	conditionnel	pr. subjonctif
vais	suis allé/e	allais	irai	irais	aille
vas	es allé/e	allais	iras	irais	ailles
va	est allé/e	allait	ira	irait	aille
allons	sommes allé/e/s	allions	irons	irions	allions
allez	êtes allé/e/s	alliez	irez	iriez	alliez
vont	sont allé/e/s	allaient	iront	iraient	aillent

impératif: va allons allez

appeler: to call

présent	passé composé	imparfait	futur	conditionnel	pr. subjonctif
appelle	ai appelé	appelais	appellerai	appellerais	appelle
appelles	as appelé	appelais	appelleras	appellerais	appelles
appelle	a appelé	appelait	appellera	appellerait	appelle
appelons	avons appelé	appelions	appellerons	appellerions	appelions
appelez	avez appelé	appeliez	appellerez	appelleriez	appeliez
appellent	ont appelé	appelaient	appelleront	appelleraient	appellent

impératif: appelle   appelons   appelez

présent	passé composé	imparfait	futur	pres. conditionnel	pr. subjonctif

apprendre: to learn

présent	passé composé	imparfait	futur	pres. conditionnel	pr. subjonctif
apprends	ai appris	apprenais	apprendrai	apprendrais	apprenne
apprends	as appris	apprenais	apprendras	apprendrais	apprennes
apprend	a appris	apprenait	apprendra	apprendrait	apprenne
apprenons	avons appris	apprenions	apprendrons	apprendrions	apprenions
apprenez	avez appris	appreniez	apprendrez	apprendriez	appreniez
apprennent	ont appris	apprenaient	apprendront	apprendraient	apprennent

impératif: apprends   apprenons   apprenez

attendre: to wait

présent	passé composé	imparfait	futur	pres. conditionnel	pr. subjonctif
attends	ai attendu	attendais	attendrai	attendrais	attende
attends	as attendu	attendais	attendras	attendrais	attendes
attend	a attendu	attendait	attendra	attendrait	attende
attendons	avons attendu	attendions	attendrons	attendrions	attendions
attendez	avez attendu	attendiez	attendrez	attendriez	attendiez
attendent	ont attendu	attendaient	attendront	attendraient	attendent

impératif: attends   attendons   attendez

avoir: to have

présent	passé composé	imparfait	futur	pres. conditionnel	pr. subjonctif
ai	ai eu	avais	aurai	aurais	aie
as	as eu	avais	auras	aurais	aies
a	a eu	avait	aura	aurait	ait
avons	avons eu	avions	aurons	aurions	ayons
avez	avez eu	aviez	aurez	auriez	ayez
ont	ont eu	avaient	auront	auraient	aient

impératif: aie   ayons   ayez

présent	passé composé	imparfait	futur	pres. conditionnel	pr. subjonctif

battre: to beat

bats	ai battu	battais	battrai	battrais	batte
bats	as battu	battais	battras	battrais	battes
bat	a battu	battait	battra	battrait	batte
battons	avons battu	battions	battrons	battrions	battions
battez	avez battu	battiez	battrez	battriez	battiez
battent	ont battu	battaient	battront	battraient	battent

impératif: bats battons battez

boire: to drink

bois	ai bu	buvais	boirai	boirais	boive
bois	as bu	buvais	boiras	boirais	boives
boit	a bu	buvait	boira	boirait	boive
buvons	avons bu	buvions	boirons	boirions	buvions
buvez	avez bu	buviez	boirez	boiriez	buviez
boivent	ont bu	buvaient	boiront	boiraient	boivent

impératif: bois buvons buvez

bouger: to move

bouge	ai bougé	bougeais	bougerai	bougerais	bouge
bouges	as bougé	bougeais	bougeras	bougerais	bouges
bouge	a bougé	bougeait	bougera	bougerait	bouge
bougeons	avons bougé	bougions	bougerons	bougerions	bougions
bougez	avez bougé	bougiez	bougerez	bougeriez	bougiez
bougent	ont bougé	bougeaient	bougeront	bougeraient	bougent

impératif: bouge bougeons bougez

| présent | passé composé | imparfait | futur | pres. conditionnel | pr. subjonctif |

changer: to change

présent	passé composé	imparfait	futur	pres. conditionnel	pr. subjonctif
change	*ai changé*	*changeais*	*changerai*	*changerais*	*change*
changes	*as changé*	*changeais*	*changeras*	*changerais*	*changes*
change	*a changé*	*changeait*	*changera*	*changerait*	*change*
changeons	*avons changé*	*changions*	*changerons*	*changerions*	*changions*
changez	*avez changé*	*changiez*	*changerez*	*changeriez*	*changiez*
changent	*ont changé*	*changeaient*	*changeront*	*changeraient*	*changent*

impératif: change   changeons   changez

chanter: to sing

présent	passé composé	imparfait	futur	pres. conditionnel	pr. subjonctif
chante	*ai chanté*	*chantais*	*chanterai*	*chanterais*	*chante*
chantes	*as chanté*	*chantais*	*chanteras*	*chanterais*	*chantes*
chante	*a chanté*	*chantait*	*chantera*	*chanterait*	*chante*
chantons	*avons chanté*	*chantions*	*chanterons*	*chanterions*	*chantions*
chantez	*avez chanté*	*chantiez*	*chanterez*	*chanteriez*	*chantiez*
chantent	*ont chanté*	*chantaient*	*chanteront*	*chanteraient*	*chantent*

impératif: chante   chantons   chantez

chercher: to look for

présent	passé composé	imparfait	futur	pres. conditionnel	pr. subjonctif
cherche	*ai cherché*	*cherchais*	*chercherai*	*chercherais*	*cherche*
cherches	*as cherché*	*cherchais*	*chercheras*	*chercherais*	*cherches*
cherche	*a cherché*	*cherchait*	*cherchera*	*chercherait*	*cherche*
cherchons	*avons cherché*	*cherchions*	*chercherons*	*chercherions*	*cherchions*
cherchez	*avez cherché*	*cherchiez*	*chercherez*	*chercheriez*	*cherchiez*
cherchent	*ont cherché*	*cherchaient*	*chercheront*	*chercheraient*	*cherchent*

impératif: cherche   cherchons   cherchez

	présent	passé composé	imparfait	futur	pres. conditionnel	pr. subjonctif

choisir : to choose

présent	passé composé	imparfait	futur	pres. conditionnel	pr. subjonctif
choisis	ai choisi	choisissais	choisirai	choisirais	choisisse
choisis	as choisi	choisissais	choisiras	choisirais	choisisses
choisit	a choisi	choisissait	choisira	choisirait	choisisse
choisissons	avons choisi	choisissions	choisirons	choisirions	choisissions
choisissez	avez choisi	choisissiez	choisirez	choisiriez	choisissiez
choisissent	ont choisi	choisissaient	choisiront	choisiraient	choisissent

impératif: choisis choisissons choisissez

commencer: to begin

présent	passé composé	imparfait	futur	pres. conditionnel	pr. subjonctif
commence	ai commencé	commençais	commencerai	commencerais	commence
commences	as commencé	commençais	commenceras	commencerais	commences
commence	a commencé	commençait	commencera	commencerait	commence
commençons	avons commencé	commencions	commencerons	commencerions	commencions
commencez	avez commencé	commenciez	commencerez	commenceriez	commenciez
commencent	ont commencé	commençaient	commenceront	commenceraient	commencent

impératif: commence commençons commencez

conduire: to drive

présent	passé composé	imparfait	futur	pres. conditionnel	pr. subjonctif
conduis	ai conduit	conduirai	conduirai	conduirais	conduise
conduis	as conduit	conduiras	conduiras	conduirais	conduises
conduit	a conduit	conduira	conduira	conduirait	conduise
conduisons	avons conduit	conduirons	conduirons	conduirions	conduisions
conduisez	avez conduit	conduirez	conduirez	conduiriez	conduisiez
conduisent	ont conduit	conduiront	conduiront	conduiraient	conduisent

impératif: conduis conduisons conduisez

présent	passé composé	imparfait	futur	pres. conditionnel	pr. subjonctif

comprendre: to understand

présent	passé composé	imparfait	futur	pres. conditionnel	pr. subjonctif
comprends	ai compris	comprenais	comprendrai	comprendrais	comprenne
comprends	as compris	comprenais	comprendras	comprendrais	comprennes
comprend	a compris	comprenait	comprendra	comprendrait	comprenne
comprenons	avons compris	comprenions	comprendrons	comprendrions	comprenions
comprenez	avez compris	compreniez	cromprendrez	comprendriez	compreniez
comprennent	ont compris	comprenaient	comprendront	comprendraient	comprennent

impératif: comprends comprenons comprenez

connaître: to know

présent	passé composé	imparfait	futur	pres. conditionnel	pr. subjonctif
connais	ai connu	connaissais	connaîtrai	connaîtrais	connaisse
connais	as connu	connaissais	connaîtras	connaîtrais	connaisses
connaît	a connu	connaissait	connaîtra	connaîtrait	connaisse
connaissons	avons connu	connaissions	connaîtrons	connaîtrions	connaissions
connaissez	avez connu	connaissiez	connaîtrez	connaîtriez	connaissiez
connaissent	ont connu	connaissaient	connaîtront	connaîtraient	connaissent

impératif: connais connaissons connaissez

continuer: to continue

présent	passé composé	imparfait	futur	pres. conditionnel	pr. subjonctif
continue	ai continué	continuais	continuerai	continuerais	continue
continues	as continué	continuais	continueras	continuerais	continues
continue	a continué	continuait	continuera	continuerait	continue
continuons	avons continué	continuions	continuerons	continuerions	continuions
continuez	avez continué	continuiez	continuerez	continueriez	continuiez
continuent	ont continué	continuaient	continueront	continueraient	continuent

impératif: continue continuons continuez

présent	passé composé	imparfait	futur	pres. conditionnel	pr. subjonctif

courir: to run

cours	ai couru	courais	courrai	courrais	coure
cours	as couru	courais	courras	courrais	coures
court	a couru	courait	courra	courrait	coure
courons	avons couru	courions	courrons	courrions	courions
courez	avez couru	couriez	courrez	courriez	couriez
courent	ont couru	couraient	courront	courraient	courent

impératif: cours courons courez

croire: to believe

crois	ai cru	croyais	croirai	croirais	croie
crois	as cru	croyais	croiras	croirais	croies
croit	a cru	croyait	croira	croirait	croie
croyons	avons cru	croyions	croirons	croirions	croyions
croyez	avez cru	croyiez	croirez	croiriez	croyiez
croient	ont cru	croyaient	croiront	croiraient	croient

impératif: crois croyons croyez

danser: to dance

danse	ai dansé	dansais	danserai	danserais	danse
danses	as dansé	dansais	danseras	danserais	danses
danse	a dansé	dansait	dansera	danserait	danse
dansons	avons dansé	dansions	danserons	danserions	dansions
dansez	avez dansé	dansiez	danserez	danseriez	dansiez
dansent	ont dansé	dansaient	danseront	danseraient	dansent

impératif: danse dansons dansez

présent	passé composé	imparfait	futur	pres. conditionnel	pr. subjonctif

demander: to ask for

demande	*ai demandé*	*demandais*	*demanderai*	*demanderais*	*demande*
demandes	*as demandé*	*demandais*	*demanderas*	*demanderais*	*demandes*
demande	*a demandé*	*demandait*	*demandera*	*demanderait*	*demande*
demandons	*avons demandé*	*demandions*	*demanderons*	*demanderions*	*demandions*
demandez	*avez demandé*	*demandiez*	*demanderez*	*demanderiez*	*demandiez*
demandent	*ont demandé*	*demandaient*	*demanderont*	*demanderaient*	*demandent*

impératif: demande   demandons   demandez

devoir: to have to/must/owe

dois	*ai dû*	*devais*	*devrai*	*devrais*	*doive*
dois	*as dû*	*devais*	*devras*	*devrais*	*doives*
doit	*a dû*	*devait*	*devra*	*devrait*	*doive*
devons	*avons dû*	*devions*	*devrons*	*devrions*	*devions*
devez	*avez dû*	*deviez*	*devrez*	*devriez*	*deviez*
doivent	*ont dû*	*devaient*	*devront*	*devraient*	*doivent*

impératif: dois   devons   devez

dire: to say

dis	*ai dit*	*disais*	*dirai*	*dirais*	*dise*
dis	*as dit*	*disais*	*diras*	*dirais*	*dises*
dit	*a dit*	*disait*	*dira*	*dirait*	*dise*
disons	*avons dit*	*disions*	*dirons*	*dirions*	*disions*
dites	*avez dit*	*disiez*	*direz*	*diriez*	*disiez*
disent	*ont dit*	*disaient*	*diront*	*diraient*	*disent*

impératif: dis   disons   dites

présent	passé composé	imparfait	futur	pres. conditionnel	pr. subjonctif

donner: to give

donne	ai donné	donnais	donnerai	donnerais	donne
donnes	as donné	donnais	donneras	donnerais	donnes
donne	a donné	donnait	donnera	donnerait	donne
donnons	avons donné	donnions	donnerons	donnerions	donnions
donnez	avez donné	donniez	donnerez	donneriez	donniez
donnent	ont donné	donnaient	donneront	donneraient	donnent

impératif: donne donnons donnez

dormir: to sleep

dors	ai dormi	dormais	dormirai	dormirais	dorme
dors	as dormi	dormais	dormiras	dormirais	dormes
dort	a dormi	dormait	dormira	dormirait	dorme
dormons	avons dormi	dormions	dormirons	dormirions	dormions
dormez	avez dormi	dormiez	dormirez	dormiriez	dormiez
dorment	ont dormi	dormaient	dormiront	dormiraient	dorment

impératif: dors dormons dormez

écouter: to listen

écoute	ai écouté	écoutais	écouterai	écouterais	écoute
écoutes	as écouté	écoutais	écouteras	écouterais	écoutes
écoute	a écouté	écoutait	écoutera	écouterait	écoute
écoutons	avons écouté	écoutions	écouterons	écouterions	écoutions
écoutez	avez écouté	écoutiez	écouterez	écouteriez	écoutiez
écoutent	ont écouté	écoutaient	écouteront	écouteraient	écoutent

impératif: écoute écoutons écoutez

présent	passé composé	imparfait	futur	pres. conditionnel	pr. subjonctif

écrire: to write

écris	ai écrit	écrivais	écrirai	écrirais	écrive
écris	as écrit	écrivais	écriras	écrirais	écrives
écrit	a écrit	écrivait	écrira	écrirait	écrive
écrivons	avons écrit	écrivions	écrirons	écririons	écrivions
écrivez	avez écrit	écriviez	écrirez	écririez	écriviez
écrivent	ont écrit	écrivaient	écriront	écriraient	écrivent

impératif: écris   écrivons   écrivez

employer: to use/employ

emploie	ai employé	employais	emploierai	emploierais	emploie
emploies	as employé	employais	emploieras	emploierais	emploies
emploie	a employé	employait	emploiera	emploierait	emploie
employons	avons employé	employions	emploierons	emploierions	employions
employez	avez employé	employiez	emploierez	emploieriez	employiez
emploient	ont employé	employaient	emploieront	emploieront	emploient

impératif: emploie   employons   employez

entendre: to hear

entends	ai entendu	entendais	entendrai	entendrais	entende
entends	as entendu	entendais	entendras	entendrais	entendes
entend	a entendu	entendait	entendra	entendrait	entende
entendons	avons entendu	entendions	entendrons	entendrions	entendions
entendez	avez entendu	entendiez	entendrez	entendriez	entendiez
entendent	ont entendu	entendaient	entendront	entendraient	entendent

impératif: entends   entendons   entendez

présent	passé composé	imparfait	futur	pres. conditionnel	pr. subjonctif

entrer: to enter

présent	passé composé	imparfait	futur	pres. conditionnel	pr. subjonctif
entre	suis entré/e	entrais	entrerai	entrerais	entre
entres	es entré/e	entrais	entreras	entrerais	entres
entre	est entré/e	entrait	entrera	entrerait	entre
entrons	sommes entré/e/s	entrions	entrerons	entrerions	entrions
entrez	êtes entré/e/s	entriez	entrerez	entreriez	entriez
entrent	sont entré/e/s	entraient	entreront	entreraient	entrent

impératif: entre entrons entrez

envoyer: to send

présent	passé composé	imparfait	futur	pres. conditionnel	pr. subjonctif
envoie	ai envoyé	envoyais	enverrai	enverrais	envoie
envoies	as envoyé	envoyais	enverras	enverrais	envoies
envoie	a envoyé	envoyait	enverra	enverrait	envoie
envoyons	avons envoyé	envoyions	enverrons	enverrions	envoyions
envoyez	avez envoyé	envoyiez	enverrez	enverriez	envoyiez
envoient	ont envoyé	envoyaient	enverront	enverraient	envoient

impératif: envoie envoyons envoyez

être: to be

présent	passé composé	imparfait	futur	pres. conditionnel	pr. subjonctif
suis	ai été	étais	serai	serais	sois
es	as été	étais	seras	serais	sois
est	a été	était	sera	serait	soit
sommes	avons été	étions	serons	serions	soyons
êtes	avez été	étiez	serez	seriez	soyez
sont	ont été	étaient	seront	seraient	soient

impératif: sois soyons soyez

présent	passé composé	imparfait	futur	pres. conditionnel	pr. subjonctif

étudier: to study

présent	passé composé	imparfait	futur	pres. conditionnel	pr. subjonctif
étudie	ai étudié	étudiais	étudierai	étudierais	étudie
étudies	as étudié	étudiais	étudieras	étudierais	étudies
étudie	a étudié	étudiat	étudiera	étudierait	étudie
étudions	avons étudié	étudiions	étudierons	étudierions	étudiions
étudiez	avez étudié	étudiiez	étudierez	étudieriez	étudiiez
étudient	ont étudié	étudiaient	étudieront	étudieraient	étudient

impératif: étudie   étudions   étudiez

faire: to do/make

présent	passé composé	imparfait	futur	pres. conditionnel	pr. subjonctif
fais	ai fait	faisais	ferai	ferais	fasse
fais	as fait	faisais	feras	ferais	fasses
fait	a fait	faisait	fera	ferait	fasse
faisons	avons fait	faisions	ferons	ferions	fassions
faites	avez fait	faisiez	ferez	feriez	fassiez
font	ont fait	faisaient	feront	feraient	fassent

impératif: fais   faisons   faites

fermer: to close

présent	passé composé	imparfait	futur	pres. conditionnel	pr. subjonctif
ferme	ai fermé	fermais	fermerai	fermerais	ferme
fermes	as fermé	fermais	fermeras	fermerais	fermes
ferme	a fermé	fermait	fermera	fermerait	ferme
fermons	avons fermé	fermions	fermerons	fermerions	fermions
fermez	avez fermé	fermiez	fermerez	fermeriez	fermiez
ferment	ont fermé	fermaient	fermeront	fermeraient	ferment

impératif: ferme   fermons   fermez

présent	passé composé	imparfait	futur	pres. conditionnel	pr. subjonctif

finir: to finish

présent	passé composé	imparfait	futur	pres. conditionnel	pr. subjonctif
finis	ai fini	finissais	finirai	finirais	finisse
finis	as fini	finissais	finiras	finirais	finisses
finit	a fini	finissait	finira	finirait	finisse
finissons	avons fini	finissions	finirons	finirions	finissions
finissez	avez fini	finissiez	finirez	finiriez	finessiez
finissent	ont fini	finissaient	finiront	finiraient	finissent

impératif: finis finissons finissez

gagner: to win/earn

présent	passé composé	imparfait	futur	pres. conditionnel	pr. subjonctif
gagne	ai gagné	gagnais	gagnerai	gagnerais	gagne
gagnes	as gagné	gagnais	gagneras	gagnerais	gagnes
gagne	a gagné	gagnait	gagnera	gagnerait	gagne
gagnons	avons gagné	gagnions	gagnerons	gagnerions	gagnions
gagnez	avez gagné	gagniez	gagnerez	gagneriez	gagniez
gagnent	ont gagné	gagnaient	gagneront	gagneraient	gagnent

impératif: gagne gagnons gagnez

garder: to keep/retain

présent	passé composé	imparfait	futur	pres. conditionnel	pr. subjonctif
garde	ai gardé	gardais	garderai	garderais	garde
gardes	as gardé	gardais	garderas	garderais	gardes
garde	a gardé	gardait	gardera	garderait	garde
gardons	avons gardé	gardions	garderons	garderions	gardions
gardez	avez gardé	gardiez	garderez	garderiez	gardiez
gardent	ont gardé	gardaient	garderont	garderaient	gardent

impératif: garde gardons gardez

Sans Détour: French for English Speakers © Copyright Gac-Artigas 1994

présent	passé composé	imparfait	futur	conditionnel	pr. subjonctif

habiter: to live in

habite	ai habité	habitais	habiterai	habiterais	habite
habites	as habité	habitais	habiteras	habiterais	habites
habite	a habité	habitait	habitera	habiterait	habite
habitons	avons habité	habitions	habiterons	habiterions	habitions
habitez	avez habité	habitiez	habiterez	habiteriez	habitiez
habitent	ont habité	habitaient	habiteront	habiteraient	habitent

impératif: habite   habitons   habitez

indiquer: to show

indique	ai indiqué	indiquais	indiquerai	indiquerais	indique
indiques	as indiqué	indiquais	indiqueras	indiquerais	indiques
indique	a indiqué	indiquait	indiquera	indiquerait	indique
indiquons	avons indiqué	indiquions	indiquerons	indiquerions	indiquions
indiquez	avez indiqué	indiquiez	indiquerez	indiqueriez	indiquiez
indiquent	ont indiqué	indiquaient	indiqueront	indiqueraient	indiquent

impératif: indique   indiquons   indiquez

interdir: to forbid

interdis	ai interdit	interdisais	interdirai	interdirais	interdise
interdis	as interdit	interdisais	interdiras	interdirais	interdises
interdit	a interdit	interdisait	interdira	interdirait	interdise
interdisons	avons interdit	interdisions	interdirons	interdirions	interdisions
interdisez	avez interdit	interdisiez	interdirez	interdiriez	interdisiez
interdisent	ont interdi	interdisaient	interdiront	interdiraient	interdisent

impératif: interdis   interdisons   interdisez

présent	passé composé	imparfait	futur	conditionnel	pr. subjonctif

jetter: to throw

jette	*ai jeté*	*jetais*	*jetterai*	*jetterais*	*jette*
jettes	*as jeté*	*jetais*	*jetteras*	*jetterais*	*jettes*
jette	*a jeté*	*jetait*	*jettera*	*jetterait*	*jette*
jetons	*avons jeté*	*jetions*	*jetterons*	*jetterions*	*jettions*
jetez	*avez jeté*	*jetiez*	*jetterez*	*jetteriez*	*jettiez*
jettent	*ont jeté*	*jetaient*	*jetteront*	*jetteraient*	*jettent*

impératif: jette   jetons   jetez

jouer: to play

joue	*ai joué*	*jouais*	*jouarai*	*jouarais*	*joue*
joues	*as joué*	*jouais*	*jouaras*	*jouarais*	*joues*
joue	*a joué*	*jouait*	*jouera*	*jouerait*	*joue*
jouons	*avons joué*	*jouions*	*jouerons*	*jouerions*	*jouions*
jouez	*avez joué*	*jouiez*	*jouerez*	*joueriez*	*jouiez*
jouent	*ont joué*	*jouaient*	*joueront*	*joueraient*	*jouent*

impératif: joue   jouons   jouez

laver: to wash

lave	*ai lavé*	*lavais*	*laverai*	*laverais*	*lave*
laves	*as lavé*	*lavais*	*laveras*	*laverais*	*laves*
lave	*a lavé*	*lavait*	*lavera*	*laverait*	*lave*
lavons	*avons lavé*	*lavions*	*laverons*	*laverions*	*lavions*
lavez	*avez lavé*	*laviez*	*laverez*	*laveriez*	*laviez*
lavent	*ont lavé*	*lavaient*	*laveront*	*laveraient*	*lavent*

impératif: lave   lavons   lavez

présent	passé composé	imparfait	futur	conditionnel	pr. subjonctif

lire: to read

présent	passé composé	imparfait	futur	conditionnel	pr. subjonctif
lis	*ai lu*	*lisais*	*lirai*	*lirais*	*lise*
lis	*as lu*	*lisais*	*liras*	*lirais*	*lises*
lit	*a lu*	*lisait*	*lira*	*lirait*	*lise*
lisons	*avons lu*	*lisions*	*lirons*	*lirions*	*lisions*
lisez	*avez lu*	*lisiez*	*lirez*	*liriez*	*lisiez*
lisent	*ont lu*	*lisaient*	*liront*	*liraient*	*lisent*

impératif: lis   lisons   lisez

louer: to rent

présent	passé composé	imparfait	futur	conditionnel	pr. subjonctif
loue	*ai loué*	*louais*	*louerai*	*louerais*	*loue*
loues	*as loué*	*louais*	*loueras*	*louerais*	*loues*
loue	*a loué*	*louait*	*louera*	*louerait*	*loue*
louons	*avons loué*	*louions*	*louerons*	*louerions*	*louions*
louez	*avez loué*	*louiez*	*louerez*	*loueriez*	*louiez*
louent	*ont loué*	*louaient*	*loueront*	*loueraient*	*louent*

impératif: loue   louons   louez

manger: to eat

présent	passé composé	imparfait	futur	conditionnel	pr. subjonctif
mange	*ai mangé*	*mangeais*	*mangerai*	*mangerais*	*mange*
manges	*as mangé*	*mangeais*	*mangeras*	*mangerais*	*manges*
mange	*a mangé*	*mangeait*	*mangera*	*mangerait*	*mange*
mangeons	*avons mangé*	*mangions*	*mangerons*	*mangerions*	*mangions*
mangez	*avez mangé*	*mangiez*	*mangerez*	*mangeriez*	*mangiez*
mangent	*ont mangé*	*mangeaient*	*mangeront*	*mangeraient*	*mangent*

impératif: mange   mangeons   mangez

présent	passé composé	imparfait	futur	conditionnel	pr. subjonctif

marcher: to walk

marche	*ai marché*	*marchais*	*marcherai*	*marcherais*	*marche*
marches	*as marché*	*marchais*	*marcheras*	*marcherais*	*marches*
marche	*a marché*	*marchait*	*marchera*	*marcherait*	*marche*
marchons	*avons marché*	*marchions*	*marcherons*	*marcherions*	*marchions*
marchez	*avez marché*	*marchiez*	*marcherez*	*marcheriez*	*marchiez*
marchent	*ont marché*	*marchaient*	*marcheront*	*marcheraient*	*marchent*

impératif: marche marchons marchez

mentir: to lie

mens	*ai menti*	*mentais*	*mentirai*	*mentirais*	*mente*
mens	*as menti*	*mentais*	*mentiras*	*mentirais*	*mentes*
ment	*a menti*	*mentait*	*mentira*	*mentirait*	*mente*
mentons	*avons menti*	*mentions*	*mentirons*	*mentirions*	*mentions*
mentez	*avez menti*	*mentiez*	*mentirez*	*mentiriez*	*mentiez*
mentent	*ont menti*	*mentaient*	*mentiront*	*mentiraient*	*mentent*

impératif: mens mentons mentez

mettre: to put

mets	*ai mis*	*mettais*	*mettrai*	*mettrais*	*mette*
mets	*as mis*	*mettais*	*mettras*	*mettrais*	*mettes*
met	*a mis*	*mettait*	*mettra*	*mettrait*	*mette*
mettons	*avons mis*	*mettions*	*mettrons*	*mettrions*	*mettions*
mettez	*avez mis*	*mettiez*	*mettrez*	*mettriez*	*mettiez*
mettent	*ont mis*	*mettaient*	*mettront*	*mettraient*	*mettent*

impératif: mets mettons mettez

Sans Détour: French for English Speakers © Copyright Gac-Artigas 1994

présent	passé composé	imparfait	futur	conditionnel	pr. subjonctif

montrer: to show

présent	passé composé	imparfait	futur	conditionnel	pr. subjonctif
montre	ai montré	montrais	montrerai	montrerais	montre
montres	as montré	montrais	montreras	montrerais	montres
montre	a montré	montrait	montrera	montrerait	montre
montrons	avons montré	montrions	montrerons	montrerions	montrions
montrez	avez montré	montriez	montrerez	montreriez	montriez
montrent	ont montré	montraient	montreront	montreraient	montrent

impératif: montre   montrons   montrez

mourir: to die

présent	passé composé	imparfait	futur	conditionnel	pr. subjonctif
meurs	suis mort(e)	mourais	mourrai	mourrais	meure
meurs	es mort(e)	mourais	mourras	mourrais	meures
meurt	est mort(e)	mourait	mourra	mourrait	meure
mourons	sommes mort(e)s	mourions	mourrons	mourrions	mourions
mourez	êtes mort(e)s	mouriez	mourrez	mourriez	mouriez
meurent	sont mort(e)s	mouraient	mourront	mourraient	meurent

impératif: meurs   mourons   mourez

naître: to be born

présent	passé composé	imparfait	futur	conditionnel	pr. subjonctif
nais	suis né(e)	naissais	naîtrai	naîtrais	naisse
nais	es né(e)	naissais	naîtras	naîtrais	naisses
naît	est né(e)	naissait	naîtra	naîtrait	naisse
naissons	sommes né(e)s	naissions	naîtrons	naîtrions	naissions
naissez	êtes né(e)s	naissiez	naîtrez	naîtriez	naissiez
naissent	sont né(e)s	naissaient	naîtront	naîtraient	naissent

impératif: nais   naissons   naissez

	présent	passé composé	imparfait	futur	conditionnel	pr. subjonctif

nourrir: to feed/nourish

présent	passé composé	imparfait	futur	conditionnel	pr. subjonctif
nourris	ai nourri	nourrissais	nourrirai	nourrirais	nourrisse
nourris	as nourri	nourrissais	nourriras	nourrirais	nourrisses
nourrit	a nourri	nourrissait	nourrira	nourrirait	nourrisse
nourrissons	avons nourri	nourrissions	nourrirons	nourririons	nourrissions
nourrissez	avez nourri	nourrissiez	nourrirez	nourririez	nourrissiez
nourrissent	ont nourri	nourrissaient	nourriront	nourriraient	nourrissent

impératif: nourris   nourrissons   nourrissez

obtenir: to get

présent	passé composé	imparfait	futur	conditionnel	pr. subjonctif
obtiens	ai obtenu	obtenais	obtiendrai	obtiendrais	obtienne
obtiens	as obtenu	obtenais	obtiendras	obtiendrais	obtiennes
obtient	a obtenu	obtenait	obtiendra	obtiendrait	obtienne
obtenons	avons obtenu	obtenions	obtiendrons	obtiendrions	obtenions
obtenez	avez obtenu	obteniez	obtiendrez	obtiendriez	obteniez
obtiennent	ont obtenu	obtenaient	obtiendront	obtiendraient	obtiennent

impératif: obtiens   obtenons   obtenez

offrir: to offer

présent	passé composé	imparfait	futur	conditionnel	pr. subjonctif
offre	ai offert	offrais	offrirai	offrirais	offre
offres	as offert	offrais	offriras	offrirais	offres
offre	a offert	offrait	offrira	offrirait	offre
offrons	avons offert	offrions	offrirons	offririons	offrions
offrez	avez offert	offriez	offrirez	offririez	offriez
offrent	ont offert	offraient	offriront	offriraient	offrent

impératif: offre   offrons   offrez

	présent	passé composé	imparfait	futur	conditionnel	pr. subjonctif

oublier: to forget

présent	passé composé	imparfait	futur	conditionnel	pr. subjonctif
oublie	ai oublié	oubliais	oublierai	oublierais	oublie
oublies	as oublié	oubliais	oublieras	oublierais	oublies
oublie	a oublié	oubliait	oubliera	oublierait	oublie
oublions	avons oublié	oubliions	oublierons	oublierions	oubliions
oubliez	avez oublié	oubliiez	oublierez	oublieriez	oubliiez
oublient	ont oublié	oubliaient	oublieront	oublieraient	oublient

impératif: oublie   oublions   oubliez

ouvrir: to open

présent	passé composé	imparfait	futur	conditionnel	pr. subjonctif
ouvre	ai ouvert	ouvrais	ouvrirai	ouvrirais	ouvre
ouvres	as ouvert	ouvrais	ouvriras	ouvrirais	ouvres
ouvre	a ouvert	ouvrait	ouvrira	ouvrirait	ouvre
ouvrons	avons ouvert	ouvrions	ouvrirons	ouvririons	ouvrions
ouvrez	avez ouvert	ouvriez	ouvrirez	ouvririez	ouvriez
ouvrent	ont ouvert	ouvraient	ouvriront	ouvriraient	ouvrent

impératif: ouvre   ouvrons   ouvrez

parler: to talk

présent	passé composé	imparfait	futur	conditionnel	pr. subjonctif
parle	ai parlé	parlais	parlerai	parlerais	parle
parles	as parlé	parlais	parleras	parlerais	parles
parle	a parlé	parlait	parlera	parlerait	parle
parlons	avons parlé	parlions	parlerons	parlerions	parlions
parlez	avez parlé	parliez	parlerez	parleriez	parliez
parlent	ont parlé	parlaient	parleront	parleraient	parlent

impératif: parle   parlons   parlez

présent	passé composé	imparfait	futur	conditionnel	pr. subjonctif

partir: to leave

présent	passé composé	imparfait	futur	conditionnel	pr. subjonctif
pars	suis parti(e)	partais	partirai	partirais	parte
pars	es parti(e)	partais	partiras	partirais	partes
part	est parti(e)	partait	partira	partirait	parte
partons	sommes parti(e)s	partions	partirons	partirions	partions
partez	êtes parti(es)s	partiez	partirez	partiriez	partiez
partent	sont parti(e)s	partaient	partiront	partiraient	partent

impératif: pars   partons   partez

payer: to pay

présent	passé composé	imparfait	futur	conditionnel	pr. subjonctif
paie	ai payé	payais	paierai	paierais	paie
paies	as payé	payais	paieras	paierais	paies
paie	a payé	payait	paiera	paierait	paie
payons	avons payé	payions	paierons	paierions	payions
payez	avez payé	payiez	paierez	paieriez	payiez
paient	ont payé	payaient	paieront	paieraient	paient

impératif: paie   payons   payez

penser: to think

présent	passé composé	imparfait	futur	conditionnel	pr. subjonctif
pense	ai pensé	pensais	penserai	penserais	pense
penses	as pensé	pensais	penseras	penserais	penses
pense	a pensé	pensait	pensera	penserait	pense
pensons	avons pensé	pensions	penserons	penserions	pensions
pensez	avez pensé	pensiez	penserez	penseriez	pensiez
pensent	ont pensé	pensaient	penseront	penseraient	pensent

impératif: pense   pensons   pensez

présent	passé composé	imparfait	futur	conditionnel	pr. subjonctif

perdre: to lose

présent	passé composé	imparfait	futur	conditionnel	pr. subjonctif
perds	ai perdu	perdais	perdrai	perdrais	perde
perds	as perdu	perdais	perdras	perdrais	perdes
perd	a perdu	perdait	perdra	perdrait	perde
perdons	avons perdu	perdions	perdrons	perdrions	perdions
perdez	avez perdu	perdiez	perdrez	perdriez	perdiez
perdent	ont perdu	perdaient	perdront	perdraient	perdent

impératif: perds   perdons   perdez

permettre: to allow

présent	passé composé	imparfait	futur	conditionnel	pr. subjonctif
permets	ai permis	permettais	permettrai	permettrais	permette
permets	as permis	permettais	permettras	permettrais	permettes
permet	a permis	permettait	permettra	permettrait	permette
permettons	avons permis	permettions	permettrons	permettrions	permettions
permettez	avez permis	permettiez	permettrez	permettriez	permettiez
permettent	ont permis	permettaient	permettront	permettraient	permettent

impératif: permets   permettons   permettez

pleurer: to cry

présent	passé composé	imparfait	futur	conditionnel	pr. subjonctif
pleure	ai pleuré	pleurais	pleurerai	pleurerais	pleure
pleures	as pleuré	pleurais	pleureras	pleurerais	pleures
pleure	a pleuré	pleurait	pleurera	pleurerait	pleure
pleurons	avons pleuré	pleurions	pleurerons	pleurerions	pleurions
pleurez	avez pleuré	pleuriez	pleurerez	pleureriez	pleuriez
pleurent	ont pleuré	pleuraient	pleureront	pleureraient	pleurent

impératif: pleure   pleurons   pleurez

présent	passé composé	imparfait	futur	conditionnel	pr. subjonctif

porter: to wear/carry

présent	passé composé	imparfait	futur	conditionnel	pr. subjonctif
porte	ai porté	portais	porterai	porterais	porte
portes	as porté	portais	porteras	porterais	portes
porte	a porté	portait	portera	porterait	porte
portons	avons porté	portions	porterons	porterions	portions
portez	avez porté	portiez	porterez	porteriez	portiez
portent	ont porté	portaient	porteront	porteraient	portent

impératif: porte portons portez

posséder: to own/master

présent	passé composé	imparfait	futur	conditionnel	pr. subjonctif
possède	ai possédé	possédais	posséderai	posséderais	possède
possèdes	as possédé	possédais	posséderas	posséderais	possèdes
possède	a possédé	possédait	possédera	posséderait	possède
possédons	avons possédé	possédions	posséderons	posséderions	possédions
possédez	avez possédé	possédiez	posséderez	posséderiez	possédiez
possèdent	ont possédé	possédaient	posséderont	posséderaient	possèdent

impératif: possède possédons possédez

pousser: to push

présent	passé composé	imparfait	futur	conditionnel	pr. subjonctif
pousse	ai poussé	poussais	pousserai	pousserais	pousse
pousses	as poussé	poussais	pousseras	pousserais	pousses
pousse	a poussé	poussait	poussera	pousserait	pousse
poussons	avons poussé	poussions	pousserons	pousserions	poussions
poussez	avez poussé	poussiez	pousserez	pousseriez	poussiez
poussent	ont poussé	poussaient	pousseront	pousseraient	poussent

impératif: pousse poussons poussez

| | présent | passé composé | imparfait | futur | conditionnel | pr. subjonctif |

pouvoir: to be able

présent	passé composé	imparfait	futur	conditionnel	pr. subjonctif
peux	ai pu	pouvais	pourrai	pourrais	puisse
peux	as pu	pouvais	pourras	pourrais	puisses
peut	a pu	pouvait	pourra	pourrait	puisse
pouvons	avons pu	pouvions	pourrons	pourrions	puissions
pouvez	avez pu	pouviez	pourrez	pourriez	puissiez
peuvent	ont pu	pouvaient	pourront	pourraient	puissent

prendre: to take

présent	passé composé	imparfait	futur	conditionnel	pr. subjonctif
prends	ai pris	prenais	prendrai	prendrais	prenne
prends	as pris	prenais	prendras	prendrais	prennes
prend	a pris	prenait	prendra	prendrait	prenne
prenons	avons pris	prenions	prendrons	prendrions	prenions
prenez	avez pris	preniez	prendrez	prendriez	preniez
prennent	ont pris	prenaient	prendront	prendraient	prennent

impératif:　　prends　　prenons　　　prenez

prêter: to lend

présent	passé composé	imparfait	futur	conditionnel	pr. subjonctif
prête	ai prêté	prêtais	prêterai	prêterais	prête
prêtes	as prêté	prêtais	prêteras	prêterais	prêtes
prête	a prêté	prêtait	prêtera	prêterait	prête
prêtons	avons prêté	prêtions	prêterons	prêterions	prêtions
prêtez	avez prêté	prêtiez	prêterez	prêteriez	prêtiez
prêtent	ont prêté	prêtaient	prêteront	prêteraient	prêtent

impératif:　　prête　　prêtons　　　prêtez

présent	passé composé	imparfait	futur	conditionnel	pr. subjonctif

recevoir: to get/receive

présent	passé composé	imparfait	futur	conditionnel	pr. subjonctif
reçois	ai reçu	recevais	recevrai	recevrais	reçoive
reçois	as reçu	recevais	recevras	recevrais	reçoives
reçoit	a reçu	recevait	recevra	recevrait	reçoive
recevons	avons reçu	recevions	recevrons	recevrions	recevions
recevez	avez reçu	receviez	recevrez	recevriez	receviez
reçoivent	ont reçu	recevaient	recevront	recevraient	reçoivent

impératif: reçois   recevons   recevez

regarder: to look at

présent	passé composé	imparfait	futur	conditionnel	pr. subjonctif
regarde	ai regardé	regardais	regarderai	regarderais	regarde
regardes	as regardé	regardais	regarderas	regarderais	regardes
regarde	a regardé	regardait	regardera	regarderait	regarde
regardons	avons regardé	regardions	regarderons	regarderions	regardions
regardez	avez regardé	regardiez	regarderez	regarderiez	regardiez
regardent	ont regardé	regardaient	regarderont	regarderaient	regardent

impératif: regarde   regardons   regardez

répondre: to answer

présent	passé composé	imparfait	futur	conditionnel	pr. subjonctif
réponds	ai répondu	répondais	répondrai	répondrais	réponde
réponds	as répondu	répondais	répondras	répondrais	répondes
répond	a répondu	répondait	répondra	répondrait	réponde
répondons	avons répondu	répondions	répondrons	répondrions	répondions
répondez	avez répondu	répondiez	répondrez	répondriez	répondiez
répondent	ont répondu	répondaient	répondront	répondraient	répondent

impératif: réponds   répondons   répondez

Sans Détour: French for English Speakers © Copyright Gac-Artigas 1994

présent	passé composé	imparfait	futur	conditionnel	pr. subjonctif

rester: to stay

reste	*suis resté/e*	*restais*	*resterai*	*resterais*	*reste*
restes	*es resté/e*	*restais*	*resteras*	*resterais*	*restes*
reste	*est resté/e*	*restait*	*restera*	*resterait*	*reste*
restons	sommes resté/e/s	*restions*	*resterons*	*resterions*	*restions*
restez	*êtes resté/e/s*	*restiez*	*resterez*	*resteriez*	*restiez*
restent	*sont resté/e/s*	*restaient*	*resteront*	*resteraient*	*restent*

impératif: reste   restons   restez

réusir: to succed

réussis	*ai réussi*	*réussissais*	*réussirai*	*réussirais*	*réussisse*
réussis	*as réussi*	*réussissais*	*réussiras*	*réussirais*	*réussisses*
réussit	*a réussi*	*réussissait*	*réussira*	*réussirait*	*réussisse*
réussissons	*avons réussi*	*réussissions*	*réussirons*	*réussirions*	*réussissions*
réussissez	*avez réussi*	*réussissiez*	*réussirez*	*réussiriez*	*réussissiez*
réussissent	*ont réussi*	*réussissaient*	*réussiront*	*réussiraient*	*réussissent*

impératif: réussis   réussissons   réussissez

rêver: to dream

rêve	*ai rêvé*	*rêvais*	*rêverai*	*rêverais*	*rêve*
rêves	*as rêvé*	*rêvais*	*rêveras*	*rêverais*	*rêves*
rêve	*a rêvé*	*rêvait*	*rêvera*	*rêverait*	*rêve*
rêvons	*avons rêvé*	*rêvions*	*rêverons*	*rêverions*	*rêvions*
rêvez	*avez rêvé*	*rêviez*	*rêverez*	*rêveriez*	*rêviez*
rêvent	*ont rêvé*	*rêvaient*	*rêveront*	*rêveraient*	*rêvent*

impératif: rêve   rêvons   rêvez

	présent	passé composé	imparfait	futur	conditionnel	pr. subjonctif

rire: to laugh

présent	passé composé	imparfait	futur	conditionnel	pr. subjonctif
ris	*ai ri*	*riais*	*rirai*	*rirais*	*rie*
ris	*as ri*	*riais*	*riras*	*rirais*	*ries*
rit	*a ri*	*riait*	*rira*	*rirait*	*rie*
rions	*avons ri*	*riions*	*rirons*	*ririons*	*riions*
riez	*avez ri*	*riiez*	*rirez*	*ririez*	*riiez*
rient	*ont ri*	*riaient*	*riront*	*riraient*	*rient*

impératif: ris   rions   riez

savoir: to know

présent	passé composé	imparfait	futur	conditionnel	pr. subjonctif
sais	*ai su*	*savais*	*saurai*	*saurais*	*sache*
sais	*as su*	*savais*	*sauras*	*saurais*	*saches*
sait	*a su*	*savait*	*saura*	*saurait*	*sache*
savons	*avons su*	*savions*	*saurons*	*saurions*	*sachions*
savez	*avez su*	*saviez*	*saurez*	*sauriez*	*sachiez*
savent	*ont su*	*savaient*	*sauront*	*sauraient*	*sachent*

impératif: sache   sachons   sachez

sentir: to feel/smell

présent	passé composé	imparfait	futur	conditionnel	pr. subjonctif
sens	*ai senti*	*sentais*	*sentirai*	*sentirais*	*sente*
sens	*as senti*	*sentais*	*sentiras*	*sentirais*	*sentes*
sent	*a senti*	*sentait*	*sentira*	*sentirait*	*sente*
sentons	*avons senti*	*sentions*	*sentirons*	*sentirions*	*sentions*
sentez	*avez senti*	*sentiez*	*sentirez*	*sentiriez*	*sentiez*
sentent	*ont senti*	*sentaient*	*sentiront*	*sentiraient*	*sentent*

impératif: sens   sentons   sentez

Sans Détour: French for English Speakers © Copyright Gac-Artigas 1994

présent	passé composé	imparfait	futur	conditionnel	pr. subjonctif

servir: to serve/be useful

présent	passé composé	imparfait	futur	conditionnel	pr. subjonctif
sers	ai servi	servais	servirai	servirais	serve
sers	as servi	servais	serviras	servirais	serves
sert	a servi	servait	servira	servirait	serve
servons	avons servi	servions	servirons	servirions	servions
servez	avez servi	serviez	servirez	serviriez	serviez
servent	ont servi	servaient	serviront	serviraient	servent

impératif: sers   servons   servez

signer: to sign

présent	passé composé	imparfait	futur	conditionnel	pr. subjonctif
signe	ai signé	signais	signerai	signerais	signe
signes	as signé	signais	signeras	signerais	signes
signe	a signé	signait	signera	signerait	signe
signons	avons signé	signions	signerons	signerions	signions
signez	avez signé	signiez	signerez	signeriez	signiez
signent	ont signé	signaient	signeront	signeraient	signent

impératif: signe   signons   signez

sortir: to go out

présent	passé composé	imparfait	futur	conditionnel	pr. subjonctif
sors	suis sorti/e	sortais	sortirai	sortirais	sorte
sors	es sorti/e	sortais	sortiras	sortirais	sortes
sort	est sorti/e	sortait	sortira	sortirait	sorte
sortons	sommes sorti/e/s	sortions	sortirons	sortirions	sortions
sortez	êtes sorti/e/s	sortiez	sortirez	sortiriez	sortiez
sortent	sont sorti/e/s	sortaient	sortiront	sortiraient	sortent

impératif: sors   sortons   sortez

	présent	passé composé	imparfait	futur	conditionnel	pr. subjonctif

souhaiter: to wish

présent	passé composé	imparfait	futur	conditionnel	pr. subjonctif
souhaite	ai souhaité	souhaitais	souhaiterai	souhaiterais	souhaite
souhaites	as souhaité	souhaitais	souhaiteras	souhaiterais	souhaites
souhaite	a souhaité	souhaitait	souhaitera	souhaiterait	souhaite
souhaitons	avons souhaité	souhaitions	souhaiterons	souhaiterions	souhaitions
souhaitez	avez souhaité	souhaitiez	souhaiterez	souhaiteriez	souhaitiez
souhaitent	ont souhaité	souhaitaient	souhaiteront	souhaiteraient	souhaitent

impératif: souhaite souhaitons souhaitez

suivre: to follow

présent	passé composé	imparfait	futur	conditionnel	pr. subjonctif
suis	ai suivi	suivais	suivrai	suivrais	suive
suis	as suivi	suivais	suivras	suivrais	suives
suit	a suivi	suivait	suivra	suivrait	suive
suivons	avons suivi	suivions	suivrons	suivrions	suivions
suivez	avez suivi	suiviez	suivrez	suivriez	suiviez
suivent	ont suivi	suivaient	suivront	suivraient	suivent

impératif: suis suivons suivez

tenir: to hold

présent	passé composé	imparfait	futur	conditionnel	pr. subjonctif
tiens	ai tenu	tenais	tiendrai	tiendrais	tienne
tiens	as tenu	tenais	tiendras	tiendrais	tiennes
tient	a tenu	tenait	tiendra	tiendrait	tienne
tenons	avons tenu	tenions	tiendrons	tiendrions	tenions
tenez	avez tenu	teniez	tiendrez	tiendriez	teniez
tiennent	ont tenu	tenaient	tiendront	tiendraient	tiennent

impératif: tiens tenons tenez

présent	passé composé	imparfait	futur	conditionnel	pr. subjonctif

toucher: to touch

présent	passé composé	imparfait	futur	conditionnel	pr. subjonctif
touche	*ai touché*	*touchais*	*toucherai*	*toucherais*	*touche*
touches	*as touché*	*touchais*	*toucheras*	*toucherais*	*touches*
touche	*a touché*	*touchait*	*touchera*	*toucherait*	*touche*
touchons	*avons touché*	*touchions*	*toucherons*	*toucherions*	*touchions*
touchez	*avez touché*	*touchiez*	*toucherez*	*toucheriez*	*touchiez*
touchent	*ont touché*	*touchaient*	*toucheront*	*toucheraient*	*touchent*

impératif: touche touchons touchez

tourner: to turn

présent	passé composé	imparfait	futur	conditionnel	pr. subjonctif
tourne	*ai tourné*	*tournais*	*tournerai*	*tournerais*	*tourne*
tournes	*as tourné*	*tournais*	*tourneras*	*tournerais*	*tournes*
tourne	*a tourné*	*tournait*	*tournera*	*tournerait*	*tourne*
tournons	*avons tourné*	*tournions*	*tournerons*	*tournerions*	*tournions*
tournez	*avez tourné*	*tourniez*	*tournerez*	*tourneriez*	*tourniez*
tournent	*ont tourné*	*tournaient*	*tourneront*	*tourneraient*	*tournent*

impératif: tourne tournons tournez

travailler: to work

présent	passé composé	imparfait	futur	conditionnel	pr. subjonctif
travaille	*ai travaillé*	*travaillais*	*travaillerai*	*travaillerais*	*travaille*
travailles	*as travaillé*	*travaillais*	*travailleras*	*travaillerais*	*travailles*
travaille	*a travaillé*	*travaillait*	*travaillera*	*travaillerait*	*travaille*
travaillons	*avons travaillé*	*travaillions*	*travaillerons*	*travaillerions*	*travaillions*
travaillez	*avez travaillé*	*travailliez*	*travaillerez*	*travailleriez*	*travailliez*
travaillent	*ont travaillé*	*travaillaient*	*travailleront*	*travailleraient*	*travaillent*

impératif: travaille travaillons travaillez

présent	passé composé	imparfait	futur	conditionnel	pr. subjonctif

traverser: to cross

traverse	ai traversé	traversais	traverserai	traverserais	traverse
traverses	as traversé	traversais	traverseras	traverserais	traverses
traverse	a traversé	traversait	traversera	traverserait	traverse
traversons	avons traversé	traversions	traverserons	traverserions	traversions
traversez	avez traversé	traversiez	traverserez	traverseriez	traversiez
traversent	ont traversé	traversaient	traverseront	traverseraient	traversent

impératif: traverse   traversons   traversez

trouver: to find

trouve	ai trouvé	trouvais	trouverai	trouverais	trouve
trouves	as trouvé	trouvais	trouveras	trouverais	trouves
trouve	a trouvé	trouvait	trouvera	trouverait	trouve
trouvons	avons trouvé	trouvions	trouverons	trouverions	trouvions
trouvez	avez trouvé	trouviez	trouverez	trouveriez	trouviez
trouvent	ont trouvé	trouvaient	trouveront	trouveraient	trouvent

impératif: trouve   trouvons   trouvez

venir: to come

viens	suis venu/e	venais	viendrai	viendrais	vienne
viens	es venu/e	venais	viendras	viendrais	viennes
vient	est venu/e	venait	viendra	viendrait	vienne
venons	sommes venu/e/s	venions	viendrons	viendrions	venions
venez	êtes venu/e/s	veniez	viendrez	viendriez	veniez
viennent	sont venu/e/s	venaient	viendront	viendraient	viennent

impératif: viens   venons   venez

	présent	passé composé	imparfait	futur	conditionnel	pr. subjonctif

voir: to see

présent	passé composé	imparfait	futur	conditionnel	pr. subjonctif
vois	ai vu	voyais	verrai	verrais	voie
vois	as vu	voyais	verras	verrais	voies
voit	a vu	voyait	verra	verrait	voie
voyons	avons vu	voyions	verrons	verrions	voyions
voyez	avez vu	voyiez	verrez	verriez	voyiez
voient	ont vu	voyaient	verront	verraient	voient

impératif: vois   voyons   voyez

vouloir: to want

présent	passé composé	imparfait	futur	conditionnel	pr. subjonctif
veux	ai voulu	voulais	voudrai	voudrais	veuille
veux	as voulu	voulais	voudras	voudrais	veuilles
veut	a voulu	voulait	voudra	voudrait	veuille
voulons	avons voulu	voulions	voudrons	voudrions	voulions
voulez	avez voulu	vouliez	voudrez	voudriez	vouliez
veulent	ont voulu	voulaient	voudront	voudraient	veuillent

impératif: veuille   veuillons   veuillez